Frederick Olumide Adetiba

EMERGING REMNANTS
—The Finishing Army—

Frederick Olumide Adetiba

EMERGING REMNANTS
the finishing army

Copyright © 2014 – Frederick Olumide Adetiba

All rights reserved. No part of this publication may be reproduced, stored in a retrieval system, or transmitted in any form or by any means – electronic, mechanical, photocopy, recording or any other – except for brief quotations in printed reviews, without the prior permission of the author.

All Scripture quotations, unless otherwise indicated, are taken from the Holy Bible: New King James Version.

Published by:
iChange Resources Limited
ichangeng@gmail.com

ISBN: 978-978-917-426-3

Contents

Dedication

Acknowledgements

Foreword

Introduction

God's Current Move in the Earth

An Army for the Finish

Basic Features

The Task

The Battlefield

The Emergence

Personal Message

Dedication

This book is dedicated to Dr. Noel Woodroffe and the entire leadership of Congress WBN across the globe, for their consistent obedience to the voice of God, and commitment to preparing the saints for the finish.

Acknowledgements

I am grateful to God for the gift of salvation and the consistent drilling and shaping I have received from Him over the years. I count it a privilege to be used to bring this book about. I am indeed nothing without Him.

I believe that we are a sum of what we have learned from all who have taught us, both great and small. Everything I have become in Christ, I owe to the men and women, young and old, that God has used to impact my life. I can boldly say that I am a product of wonderful men and women God has brought my way at different seasons of my life, many of whom I may not capture here.

I am particularly grateful to Dr. Noel Woodroffe, the president of Congress WBN and the senior elder of Elijah Centre, Trinidad and Tobago. This work is a product of your continuous access to the intent and purposes of God per time. To my senior elder and pastor of New Tribes Assembly, Abuja, Engr. Brendy Mba; thank you for providing me with a cover when I needed it the most. You also gave me the impetus to complete this work. Your editorial input and contributions are invaluable.

I also want to appreciate the senior elder of Knesset Community Abuja, Prince Omola Geoffrey, for taking time to go through this work and making invaluable clarifications and suggestions. Thank you to Mrs. Nkiru Brendy, Big John, Dickson, Ijeoma, Mr. & Mrs. Adeyemi, Mr. & Mrs. Gozie Okoroafor, Vincent, Paul, Sis. Debby, Kennedy, Favour, Victor, Abel, Sunday Omotolu, John & Loveth Anejo, Odunayo, Bolaji, Yinka, Odion, Ina and all my other folks in Knesset Community and New Tribes Assembly, Abuja. A special gratitude goes to my boss, my teacher, my friend and mentor, Dapo Olorunyomi. Thank you for believing in me and encouraging me to do many amazing things. And to Ben Atuluku for your encouragement and helping to see this project through.

My appreciation goes to Dr. Emmanuel Kanos, Setman and Senior Pastor of the Parliament, Jos. It was a rare privilege to be tutored by you. To a mentor and a teacher, Professor Victor Dugga, words are not enough to describe how much you have impacted my life and everyone who has crossed path with you. To all the Pastors and members of the Parliament, Jos and Abuja, I am glad to be part of the marathon spiritual development we all went through. And to all the members of Youth for The Nations Ministry (Club 8-2), with whom I started this journey, God bless you all.

My profound gratitude goes to my friends and colleagues, who made invaluable editorial input, and others for their encouragement: Elor Nkereuwem, Tobi Oluwatola, Dotun Eyinade, Seun Fakuade, Obiwon, Willie Obase-Ota, Deshola Komolafe, Omena Abenabe, Ebi Dressman, Ibijoke Faseun (friend & partner) and several others.

A special appreciation goes to Pastor & Mrs. Umoru. Thank you for believing in me and for your unflinching support. To Arch. Shola Adetiba, Olu Bolus, Mr & Mrs Michael Lawal, Taiye and Kehinde, Biodun, Iyabo, Dele and the entire Lawals family. To my parents, and my siblings: Dotun, Mrs. Bukola Faloju, Ayo, Kola, Feyi, Lola, Victor and Sammy. To the entire Bolus, Olubos and Adetibas family, and many others not mentioned; you have all contributed to this work in one way or another. Thank you and God bless.

Foreword

Some write books because they are scholars and are thus trained to write; just to contribute to the body of knowledge, while some others write about what they are dynamically experiencing and/or interacting with. Mine has been the singular opportunity to have both proofread this work as a manuscript (which painfully took a long time because of obvious constraints), and observed the kernel of the message in this book demonstrated in the life of Fred as his pastor.

Emerging Remnants encapsulates what I see as the current emphasis of God to His Church in these ultimate days of mortal existence. This current divine mind has taken a while to crystallize into our spiritual clime, as is usual with the processes of truth. However, we have arrived at the stage of this truth where clichés like "The last day army", "the last great move of God", and "the final revival", etc., have taken hold of the Church with Babel of confusing perspectives. 1 Corinthians 14:8 (NKJV) - *"For if the trumpet makes an uncertain sound, who will prepare himself for battle?"* This book is a certain sound of the trumpet, which has the capacity to both arouse and stir this generation for battle. It sparks with clarity all through its pages.

There is a bigger purpose to (your) life- it is not all about you; it is all about God. This life is a dress rehearsal to the real life that is yet to come. Assessment of true life should be from unseen values. We are on a journey in and to God, from the day we embraced the grace of God in Christ. This journey has a destination: it is not endless. As we approach the end, process has to become more precise, exact and adjusted properly by the destination. Options are less tolerated – the trajectory of my personal life, ministry initiatives and activities, leadership structure, etc., must all become more exact and more correct.

This little book in your hand can make your entire life (priority, pursuit, emphasis) more precise, exact and accurately adjusted to line up with our destination. "The bride must make herself ready for her wedding". It requires far more than just joining the bandwagon of proclaimers, who seldom even understand the content of their proclamation and its ramification. Fred takes us through the grasping of the context and content of the current emphasis of God, through the rudiments of the requirements to be enlisted in the army, to what the task ahead of us is and where the battlefield really is.

Old religious stereotypes, rigid categorizations, and fossilised revelation parameters, are issues that we must confront and be delivered from in order to be enlisted in this army. The hardest area of death to self is death to old fossilised religious positions; however, it is the true path to a new day in God. I strongly recommend this book to every serious minded believer who genuinely desires to see the glory of the latter house eclipsing that of the former. Out of the ashes of our dying today, we will see the breaking forth of a brand new day.

Brendy Ndukwe
Senior Elder,
New Tribes Assembly, Abuja.

Introduction

Emerging Remnants is a product of series of dealings that began in early 2000, when I was just a tender believer. It was a period of spiritual breakthrough for me, resulting from my coming into the Apostolic/Prophetic Reformation through Dr. Noel Woodroffe[1], the president of Congress WBN. Prior to that time, I had never conceived the idea of writing a book, especially one such as this.

The focus of earlier inner transactions was on the subject of *leadership* in the Church and in my country, Nigeria. However, as I began to have a broader and in-depth understanding of the issues God was raising in my spirit, I discovered it was not just about leadership, but more about the Kingdom of God and His end time agenda, which will ultimately set the stage for bringing this age to a close.

It also became clear that it has to do with the broad intention of God for me and my generation, and that broad intention is the emergence of His Army; a new species of the human race (enhanced humanness), that will accelerate the fulfillment of His purposes in the earth, thereby establishing His rule in every area of human life and existence. What sets them apart as a new species of human race is the abandonment of their own will, commitment to spiritual development and growth into Christ-likeness, and focus on accomplishing divine intents and purposes.

In order to successfully attain the finish, it is important to understand where we are coming from, our current location, and how we got to where we are; what I call the spiritual development of the Church. There has been a progressive movement and restoration of truths in the Body of Christ that every believer needs to be able to track. This book attempts to provide an overview of that movement.

---

[1] Dr. Noel Woodroffe is the President of Congress WBN, a network of Churches and other initiatives spread across over 90 countries.

There is also a focus on Nigeria as one of the geographical epicenters of these unfolding events. This means that Nigeria is one of the pivotal nations where God's plan will be fully expressed in this season. God's programme for the end is a global phenomenon but it will find expression in different ways across the nations (geographical delineations).

This book represents a fragment of understanding of God's global purpose for this season. There are other works and speakers who have provided insights from other perspectives. You will find a comprehensive Bible reference which was intended to provide access to the major scriptural quotations in the book. Endeavour to also search the Scripture for other passages quoted.

As you read along, I hope it will confirm some dealings of God in your life, and, most importantly, spur you to start making quality decisions regarding your relationship with God, vis-à-vis what He is currently doing in the earth. I challenge you to seek to have comprehensive understanding of the plans of God concerning **THE FINISH**, as well as your individual stake in it.

CHAPTER ONE

GOD'S CURRENT MOVE IN THE EARTH

In late 20th century, God initiated a major advance in the spirit, captured as a move of God. Those who were sensitive to the voice of the Spirit and were ready to journey received it and responded accordingly (John 10:27). This call to move became clearer and gained prominence at the dawn of the 21st century. Without a doubt, it was a *trumpet blast* that signaled an advance into the next level of divine purpose.

Expectedly, people responded and are still responding to this call differently. The different reactions so far can be categorized as follows:

The Initial Ignorant Majority

This category is made up of people who are totally oblivious of what is happening. They have no clue yet that God is doing something new. To this vast majority, it is religious business as usual. I believe, in one way or another, the true God seekers amongst them will have the opportunity to come into this understanding. Diligent seekers will always find God (Proverbs 8:17, Amos 5:4, Jeremiah 29:13 – AMP). I was part of this ignorant majority until my privileged encounter with this truth.

The Naïve

The second category is made up of those who are aware but too simple minded to make the necessary transactions to heed the call and move in the new direction God is leading His people. These ones have heard or read about it, but cannot not take the initiative to ask God for clarity and direction because they are too engrossed in the old position they are familiar with. These are like the disciples of Christ that turned away from Him when He demanded they look beyond satisfying their mortal desires (John 6:48-67).

I once met a pastor who after our discussion along this line was in agreement that God was indeed doing something new. He however maintained that this level of truth was not meant for everybody. What I was hearing him say in other words was, "You guys go ahead and press into the deeper things of God; some of us are meant to remain at our located comfort zone."

The Rebellious

This category of respondents is made up people who are mainly the custodians of the old order. They know very well about the new demands of the Spirit, but because it would require they move from their comfort zone, and lose their religious titles and positions in some instances, they are not willing to let go. Instead, like the Pharisees and Sadducees in the days of Jesus, they vehemently stand against the call to advance. These are like the segment of Israelites who kept craving for garlic and cucumber of Egypt, while on their way to the Promised Land. They prefer the old positions that have become their comfort zone.

For instance, some friends with whom we came into this truth gave up even before the journey started. They said this new level of truth would prevent them from pursuing their personal ambition for fame and wealth. And they went back to the old and popular spiritual position that gives room for pursuit of personal ambition. These guys had a glimpse of the requirements for the attainment of this new spiritual height. As you will see in subsequent chapters, this new spiritual position requires we die to self and fleshly-motivated ambitions.

Today, some of these folks are no longer in the faith. They are neck-deep in Babylon, competing with the world for wealth and fame, which popular Christianity also gives room for.

Insufficient Knowledge

These are people with insufficient knowledge of the ways of God. They express this by maintaining that God cannot be doing anything new; that God does not move. The move of God in this sense does not mean God Himself is moving or changing, because He is the definition of existence and the Unchanging Essence. What this implies is that God is moving His people to another level in Himself. And He is the one leading us.

What vast majority of believers seems to be finding difficult to grapple with is that the dealings of God with man are progressive. God is not literally changing base or position, but His emphases and operations, in the earth, are progressive. God is currently operating in a whole new frequency, and it takes only those whose antennas are tuned to that dimension and are kingdom minded to know His current emphases. This progressive operation buttresses the fact that God is involved in a building construction. And we are the building (1 Corinthians 3:9). Jesus Christ also implied this in Matthew 16:18, when He said: "...I will **build** my church..." (Emphasis is mine).

THE WORD AS DIVINE BUILDING BLOCK
The principal raw material God uses in this construction is His word. The building and restoration of man is the greatest significance of the word of God. We have the written word as well as the spoken word for this purpose. There are seasons when God issues landmark commands (word) to accelerate the building process. Just as builders cannot lay all the bricks of a building in one day, even if they are available, typifies how God is building us. If the builder decides to lay all the bricks in one day because they are available, the building would most likely crumble that same day. Every form of construction goes through a process. It has to be step by step; allowing the previous layers to firm up and stay strong before laying the others. By following the systematic process, the building would stand strong.

There are some things in the heart of God for us that we cannot comprehend and implement at once. He has decided to package and release them to us in bits and chunks. God spoke to Jeremiah in this light saying, "Call to me and I will answer you and show you great and mighty things which you do not know" (Jeremiah 33:3). Jesus Christ also told the disciples that He had many more things to tell them that they could not bear at the time. He however promised them the Holy Spirit, whose function among many others would be to grant them access to those things (John 16:12-13). The Holy Spirit is still performing this function in our day; granting us access to deeper truths that were hidden from previous generations.

God has given us the written word while still speaking to us. His spoken word unpacks and activates the written word. We must depend on these two dimensions of His word for our lives to be built. The written word is even deadly without the activation of the Holy Spirit through the spoken word. That is why Paul clearly stated that "the letter kills, but the Spirit gives life" (2 Corinthians 3:6). The spoken word helps to unlock the principles behind the written word. If not for this understanding, we would have continued to sacrifice bulls and other prescribed animals for the atonement of our sins.

While the written word, as contained in the Bible, remains the accurate and adequate reference point and fundamental truth for our advance in this journey, it does not contain all the experiences our fathers had of God in literal sense. John who had a more elaborate account of the life of Jesus Christ pointed out that there were several things He did that were not documented (John 21:25). This realization ought to propel us to press deeper into God's truth through the help of the Holy Spirit. Our truth-seeking must be guided and led by the Holy Spirit. Those who by-pass the Holy Spirit and the written word to seek truth usually end up in spiritism and various spiritistic experiences that are not from God. This unguided truth-seeking gave birth to some African traditional "Christian" practices in Nigeria, and several new age religions across the world.

It was in the context of the spoken word that Jesus Christ responded to Satan when He was tempted: "...*Man shall not live by bread alone, but by every word that **proceeds** from the mouth of God*" (Matthew 4:4). The key word in the passage is the tense PROCEEDS, which is a present continuous tense. This shows clearly that God speaks. His speaking (prophetic instructions and admonitions) is progressive, indicative of the building process. It is difficult to believe that some people actually think God's speaking to the Church stopped with the early Apostles. Some of these people in contrast to Ephesians 4:9-13, do not believe there are functional apostolic and prophetic, and by extension, evangelistic, pastoral and teaching graces in the Church today. God has been speaking and will continue to speak until this building process is completed. These five-fold gifts are required for the Church to attain maturity.

When man fell, he lost an important dimension (the nature) of God. Regaining what was lost is what has taken the form of a building process or a journey. The speaking of God brings clarity, new and up-to-date understanding of what was written, and the time for their accomplishment. Our engagement with these current positions in God is indicative of our advancement in Him, which is simply taking the form of the design that exists in His heart right here on earth. To put this more succinctly, the Church is on a journey, and our destination is that place which is defined by God's original intention for man. We are simply journeying back to God through Christ.

It is also important for us to understand that this journey is a spiritual experience. God demonstrated this spiritual experience with the children of Israel, when they had to move from Goshen in Egypt to Canaan, the Promised Land. Apart from being a place of slavery (bondage, ineptitude, darkness, cluelessness), Goshen also represents an obsolete position where the people lacked the capacity to be who God had designed them to be. Paul noted that the wilderness experience is a pattern for us - the New Testament believers (1 Corinthians 10:1-11). This means that the physical migration of the children of Israel is our preordained spiritual reality. We will see in subsequent chapters that this mindset (journeying/pilgrimage) is a requirement for those who will take the purposes of God to the FINISH.

The best word that has been used by and large to describe or capture what God is doing in the earth today is the word REFORMATION. The word has its root in the Greek word DIORTHOSIS, which is a branch of medical science that deals with the re-structuring of the internal skeletal frame of human in order to give it an accurate outer form. It deals with bone structure that has misaligned, which, by implication, affects the posture or movement. Our mindset, our doctrinal emphasis, our eschatological positions, and our internal spiritual postures reflect how we operate and how we represent and express God in the earth. To accurately represent God, these internal postures need re-structuring with the prophetic revelation and apostolic truth position. This is what God is doing in this season.

Internal structural adjustment, as we may wish to see it, is necessary at this point in time in order for the Church to get back on track with God. This is because we have stayed at this stale position for too long. So many truths have become corrupted, thereby affecting our posture and relevance in the earth. Without these adjustments, the Church will remain incapacitated to take God's purposes to a defined conclusion, and the finish will remain an illusion irrespective of how much we talk or sing about it. God has raised and He is still in the enterprise of raising great and dedicated men to blow the trumpet for an advance.

UNDERSTANDING THE RESTORATION MOVES OF GOD
The Church, which started with the twelve apostles, was formally birthed on the day of Pentecost (Acts 2). At that time, there was a great manifestation of the Holy Spirit as promised by Jesus Christ. This was followed by an extended period of persecution, after which the Church went under, during the Dark Ages. This period, which is also known in history as the "Medieval Period" or the "Middle Ages", spanned about 300 years. It was at that time that the State and the Church were fused together which saw to the perversion of foundational truths upon which the Church was built.

At the end of the 300 years of darkness and corruption of the word, God began to restore vital truths back to the Church. These vital truths are bricks God is using to build the Church. That has been the core reality of the believer as Jesus Christ continues to build the Church.

The 21st century reformation which is known as the APOSTOLIC REFORMATION or the APOSTOLIC/PROPHETIC REFORMATION has been conceptualized differently by different people. While it is important to have appropriate concepts and terminologies to describe the movement of God in the earth, which helps our understanding, our ability to capture the spirit (essence) of these moves is of utmost importance. There are people in this current move who have captured the language and terminologies but have left the spirit (essence) behind.

It important to clarify that this current move of God is not a mere restoration of truth, but a reformation. This usually comes with tearing down old structures that no longer have the capacity to accommodate the present demands of the Spirit or serve the purposes of God. A close example of what we have today is the reformation that took place during the time of our Lord Jesus Christ, when the Church was in her formative stage. When Jesus came, there was an existing Mosaic order that was led by the Pharisees which had to give way because of its inaccuracies and inability to access the heart of God for the season.

The Apostolic and Prophetic Reformation is an all-encompassing move, with the capacity to prepare the saints for the battle of the end, and for the fulfillment of the purposes of God in the earth. One of the significant features it came with is the restoration of the office of the apostle, which is the last of the five-fold gifts to be restored since the Church went into the Dark Ages.

> *And He Himself gave some to be apostles, some prophets, some evangelists, some pastors and teachers, for the equipping of the*

saints for the work of the ministry for the edifying of the body of Christ... (Ephesians 4:11).

In the course of restoring other vital truths since the 16th century, other gifts (offices) of the Teacher, Pastor, Evangelist and Prophet were restored. The office of the apostle was given first (1 Corinthians 12:28), and became the last to be restored.

The activation of the office of the Apostle is very important for the Church to attain maturity and become all that Jesus Christ intended. In Ephesians 2:20, the Bible says that the Church is built on the foundation of the apostles and prophets. The working together of these two offices in alignment with the others is very crucial in the maturity of the saints and the building of the Church. The saints can only be accurately trained and equipped for the work of the ministry in the last days when we have the entire five-fold gifts working together. The relationship between them is not that of dependence but interdependence. The five offices will have to work in tandem to fulfill God's ultimate plan for this season.

Today, a lot of people go around with different titles that have little or nothing to do with what they do in reality. The office of the apostle is not just about the title but the calling, commissioning and functionality in the grace and anointing of the apostolic. Same goes for the office of the prophet and the other gifts. Apostle Paul repeatedly introduced himself as one called and commissioned into the office of the apostle (Romans 1:1, 1 Corinthians 1:1, 2 Corinthians 1:1, Ephesians 1:1, Colossians 1:1). His functionality in that capacity helped to build the early Church, which is equally relevant in the maturation of the finishing Church.

The work of the apostle among other things is to build structures to give physical expression to the intents and desires of God as revealed through the prophet. Those who have been commissioned to operate in that capacity are endowed with apostolic grace and wisdom to design blueprints for the execution of divine intents. They are graced to build accurate patterns in local assemblies, and also correct errors by establishing proper order and structure (1 Corinthians 3:10). This we see Paul doing in the course of his missionary journey, and which can be clearly seen in the Corinthian Church in particular (the first epistle to the Corinthians).

The table below provides some insights into the restored truths since the Dark Ages, with dates and the people God used to pioneer them:

Source: Congress WBN 2002[2]

DATE	RESTORED TRUTH	SOME OF THE PIONEERS
Early 1500s	Justification by Faith	Martin Luther, William Thindale, John Calvin
1600s	Water Baptism	The AnaBaptist: Menno Simons(Europe), Rogel Williams (USA)
1700s	Holiness, Sanctification and Perfectionism	The Wesley Brothers – John
1800s	Divine Faith Healings	Alexander Dowie, Maria Woodworth-Ether
1900s	Holy Ghost Baptism and Other Tongues	William Seymour
1940s	Laying on of Hands and Personal Prophecies	Oral Roberts, Paul Cain
1950s	Charismatic Renewal	Demos Shakarian, Kathryn Kulman
1960s	Demonology, Obsession, Oppression, Possession (DELIVERANCE)	Derek Prince, Bill Subrisky
Early 1970s	Discipleship, Family Life Church Growth	Yonggi Cho, Bill Bright
Late 1970s	Faith Message, Prosperity, Word Teaching	Kenneth Hagin, Ken Copeland, Fred Price, Benson Idahosa...
Early 1980s	Global Prayer Movement	Peter Wagner, Cindy Jacobs, Emeka Nwankpa
Mid 1980s	Dominion, Prophetic Movement	Bill Hamon
Early 1990s	**Prophetic/Apostolic Dimension**	**Bill Hamon, Rick Joyner, Noel Woodroffe, Paul Humberstone, John Singleton, Robert Munien...**

---

[2] This table was gotten from the back page of 2002 Congress WBN Nigeria Reformation Conference publicity material. Congress WBN then was called World Breakthrough Network (WBN).

This table is not exhaustive, but it gives us an idea of the spiritual journey of the Church from the Dark Ages. A closer look at the table would reveal that it reflects the different emphases that characterise the church world today. Majority of local assemblies (denominations) that we have today are differentiated along the line of restored truths, particularly up until 1980s. Irrespective of the name, the emphasis is one or a combination of faith messages, prosperity, holiness, deliverance, healing, prayer, word teaching etc. The overriding emphasis always reflects in the messages and programmes. This is what is responsible for the current schism and sectionalism in the Church.

This is more so because different church leaders tapped into different emphases and decided to camp there, and are unwilling to move into new depths in God. Over time that position becomes their comfort zone. Even when God begins to emphasise a current truth position, they are usually too engrossed in the old position to migrate. That is also what gives rise to some of the different reactions of people to this current move of God as explained earlier.

It is not wise to hold on to the old emphasis when God begins to release new truths, when we are expected to imbed these truths and move on with God. This comfort zone may produce large congregations and other manifestations of miracles, signs and wonders, but it will not be able to bring God's purposes to the finish. That is why we have so many 'christians', many 'church assemblies', many 'pastors', loads of miracles and manifestations, yet our society (Nigeria) is ridden with injustice, corruption, poverty and other ills. There is no commensurate impact. The overarching emphasis of popular Christianity is meeting the material needs of the people, while paying very little emphasis on what God wants the people to do and become.

By focusing on the needs of the people at the expense who they need to become and what they need to do, they are denied the awesome opportunity of partnering with God to close this age. Moves of God are powered the Holy

Spirit, but are usually driven by human component in the earth. Nothing happens if there is no human component partnering with the Holy Spirit to make it happen. As noted somewhere in this book, this is simply a privilege God has accorded man, because there is absolutely nothing He cannot do. These humans facilitators are usually the remnants who look forward to, long for and demand for deeper dimensions of God in their days. For instance, we had Simeon and Anna (Luke 2:25-28), who facilitated the coming of Jesus Christ, as well as the ordinary folks who carried on the work after His death, some of whom later became the Apostles.

THE NATURE OF APOSTOLIC REFORMATION
One of the unique features of the present Apostolic Reformation of the Church is that it requires a paradigm shift. A paradigm can be equated with the operating system of a computer which helps to run different programmes. Without the operating system, programmes cannot run on the modern computers, and without an upgraded operating system the computer will not also run some recently developed programmes.

The concept, paradigm shift was introduced by scientist, Thomas Kuhn[3]. He defines it as the constellation of beliefs, values and techniques shared by members of a given community. The paradigm we operate with defines and shapes the emphases and outcomes of our activities. To effectively operate at the level where God is right now (in the Apostolic Reformation), there has to be a paradigm shift from the old position. In this context, a paradigm would also mean mindset or mentality.

The mindset of the prevailing order cannot drive the demands of the emerging Apostolic and Prophetic Reformation. The mindset of the average believer today is what he/she can get from God. The emphasis is centred on self, as against dying to self and seeking to know and do the will of the Father.

---

[3] Thomas Kuhn. (2014, July 11). In *Wikipedia, The Free Encyclopedia*. Retrieved 19:44, August 24, 2014, from http://en.wikipedia.org/w/index.php?title=Thomas_Kuhn&oldid=616527657

Miracles, deliverance, prosperity, breakthroughs are some of the things that the average believer is after. These things are not wrong in themselves, but they cannot be the object of our worship and service to God anymore. Promoting them cannot serve the ultimate purpose of God. This may have been permitted at a time; it is no longer the focus. The focus now is advancing the frontiers of the Kingdom of God until we arrive at the finish.

The mentality of serving God just to have our needs met is like that of a child who needs incentives for good behaviour. In child psychology, it is called positive reinforcements. A time comes when the child is expected to become matured and responsible. Only a dysfunctional grown man would require positive reinforcements to behave appropriately. This equally applies in the Kingdom. God expects us to grow to maturity. As long as the believers continue to dwell on these benefits (the 'bless me before...' or 'bless me or else...' mentality), they cannot take the purposes of God to the finish. Little wonder Jesus Christ described healing as the children's bread (Matthew 15:22-26).

God wants to give us the Kingdom (Luke 12:32), but we seem to prefer the crumbs that fall off the table. Because we are too earthly and carnal, we pay very little attention to more glorious dimension of what God has in store for us. What we are taking for granted is what our heroes of faith lived and sacrificed earthly pleasure for, but still did not attain, because God had something better for us (Hebrews 11). If we are going to step into this glorious life that God has planned for us here on earth, then like our progenitors (heroes of faith), we must discountenance this earth and situate our life's endeavours and pursuits within God's ultimate plan and purpose.

The accurate mindset in this season is that which seeks to know what is in the heart of the Father and to do it. The emphasis can no longer be what we can get from Him but what He requires of us to do. It is time we recognized that we are tools in His hands to fulfill His intentions. The material benefits such as prosperity, financial breakthroughs, and immaterial benefits such as deliverance, healing miracles etc., are means to an end and fringe benefits of the seed of God that is developing within us. Unfortunately, we have made them an end in themselves. Some believers even go as far as using their possession as a sign of God's approval or His presence in their lives. This is a great deception from the pit of hell because some unbelievers even enjoy these things in greater proportion.

This was the mindset of some disciples of Christ who were going after Him for their needs, including fish and bread. At the point where He talked to them about eating His flesh and drinking His blood which simply means having a part of Him (sharing His life, purpose and suffering), the Bible recorded that many of His disciples left Him (John 6). They said it was a hard saying (a sign of immaturity).

Anyone without an accurate (required) mindset cannot operate in this present move of God. The old mindset and structures have to be done away with. A new mindset and structures are needed to operate in this new season. Jesus Christ talking to His disciples said:

> *No one puts a piece of unshrunk cloth on an old garment; for the patch pulls away from the garment, and the tear is made worse. Nor do they put new wine into old wineskins, or else the wineskins break, the wine is spilled, and the wineskins are ruined. But they put new wine into new wineskins, and both are preserved* – Matthew 9:16, 17

In the old moves, everything seems to be about the self. But in this season, everything is about God. All endeavours and activities of the Church in this season must be directed towards the establishment and advancement of the Kingdom. This simply means the lordship of God in every sphere of human life on earth. This starts with the submission of the totality of our lives to God's authority. There has to be the expression of the Kingdom of God within us first before we can impart the world with it. This also comes with purging ourselves of the elements of the world.

LEADERSHIP

Leadership is an important aspect of what God is doing in this season. Effective leadership is the ability to lead a people from a defined unpleasant and stale position to a more suitable and preferred state. The impact of leadership can therefore be assessed by looking at the conditions of the people over a given period of time. A panoptic look at global affairs shows that humanity is at the brink and leadership failure accounts for the majority of these crises.

The current social, political and economic problems facing the African continent today can be attributed to leadership failure. Majority of their population live in poverty and other forms of social vices despite the enormous resources God has blessed them with. There is no amount of wealth a country can possess that will make any meaningful impact in the lives of the people if there are no good leaders to properly manage them. No society can attain meaningful development (a development that is centred on the well-being of the ordinary people and not just economic indicators) without a committed and dedicated leadership. This is exactly the problem with Nigeria, and other Third World countries.

It is important to note that these leaders are products of the society, which is why we see successive generations operating below the standard of their predecessors rather than surpassing it. It is only in exceptional cases that you see successive leaders outperforming their predecessors. This clearly means that the situation is not getting better. And this can be attributed to the fact that current leaders have been passing on their defective notion of leadership to their successors, either consciously or unconsciously. The younger generations in turn aggravate the situation, and the vicious cycle continues. In Nigeria for instance, everyone seems to want their share of the 'national cake'. Public service at all levels has become opportunity for accumulation of wealth by the few who get to occupy them, at the expense of the vast majority of the people.

The youths who represent the future, and are referred to the leaders of tomorrow are further endangered because of dearth of good role models. The average young person is also looking for the opportunity to loot from the public purse, rather than turn things around for the better. Everybody seems to be waiting in turn to destroy the system for their selfish desires. This vicious cycle has become entrenched into the system. It's now a case of 'you can't beat them; just join them'. It will however take a radical departure from the norm to break the ugly trend.

The Church has also not fared better in this regard. Leadership patterns that are prevalent in the world are gradually finding their way into the Church. Now we see politics as being practised in the world in some churches that have become like corporations. It is no longer uncommon to see pastors surround themselves with heavy protocol and security details like our politicians, making them inaccessible to the ordinary members of their congregations. Opulence and ostentatious living has become the order of the day for some, while the majority of their members wallow in abject poverty.

Paul described the Church as "the ground and pillar of truth" (1 Timothy 3:15). The Church is supposed to be a reference point for leadership. The inability of the Church to maintain this position is among the reasons why God initiated a reformation in order to raise a new generation that will show forth His nature, character and intents, and bring the Church to her true place of relevance and significance in the earth.

Leadership has erroneously been conceived as an opportunity to exploit and live off the people that are being led. In Nigeria particularly, leadership is seen as an opportunity for primitive accumulation of wealth at all levels and in every sphere. There is oppression and domination of the people by the leaders.

And those positions are seen as opportunity to exploit the same people they are meant to serve.

What we have now is some pastors practically living off the people. Although, the Bible encourages us to give to those who bless us spiritually, what we have today is multiple exploitation of the people. They preach messages that sometimes manipulate their congregations in the name of prosperity and having their problems solved. These messages have led some people into sharp practices that have made headlines in time past, bringing the Church of Christ to disrepute and ridicule. Prophet Ezekiel was confronted with a similar situation in his day. The state of affairs at that time as described is typical of what we have today:

> *Son of man, prophesy against the shepherds of Israel, prophesy and say to them, "Thus says the Lord God to the shepherds of Israel who feed themselves! Should not the shepherd feed the flocks? You eat the fat and clothe yourselves with the wool; you slaughter the fatlings, but you have not fed the flock. The weak you have not strengthened, nor have healed those who were sick, nor bound what is broken and brought back what was driven away, nor sought what was lost; but with force and cruelty you have ruled them... Ezekiel 34:2-4*

It is important to realize that God will not fold His arms and let this continue. His judgment will come upon these leaders as in the days of Ezekiel:

> *...I am against the shepherds, and I will require My flock at their hand; I will cause them to cease feeding the sheep, and the shepherds shall feed themselves no more; for I will deliver my flock from their mouths, that they may no longer be food for them. Ezekiel 34:10*

The display of opulence by our pastors has created the notion of lucrative 'church business'. Many people who were never called into any of the five-fold ministries have now taken to the pulpit as a way of survival. They go about with different high-sounding titles, and doing more damage to the people. You usually find them in major cities, preying on gullible people, especially women. Paul commented on their activities in his second letter to Timothy (2 Timothy 3:1-6).

REDEFINING LEADERSHIP

Warped understanding of leadership accounts for the numerous problems faced by the Church and the society at large today. In the 21st century however, the Emerging Remnants will restore and exemplify the true meaning of leadership, both in the Church and in the world system where they will function. The kingdom conception and practice of leadership will liberate the people from oppression and exploitation. This will confirm the statement that: "When the righteous are in authority, the people rejoice..."- Proverbs 29:2.

Central to the kingdom definition of leadership is **SERVICE**. Leaders are called to serve the people and not the other way around as is common in our society today. This definition of leadership is summarized in the teaching of Jesus Christ Himself when James and John secretly asked for a place of honour in His Kingdom:

> *When the ten other disciples discovered what James and John had asked, they were indignant. So Jesus called them together and said, "You know that in this world kings are tyrants, and officials lord it over the people beneath them. But among you it should be quite different. Whoever wants to be a leader among you must be your servant, and whoever wants to be first must be the slave of all. For even I, the Son of man, came here not to be served but to serve others, and give my life as a ransom for many. – Mark 10:41-45 (NLT)*

The kernel of kingdom leadership is the **PEOPLE**. Whenever God calls a man, He has a people in mind. The people therefore must be paramount in the heart of the leader. This was clearly demonstrated by Jesus Christ. We also see these qualities in the leadership of Paul, Moses and others. When God called Moses, He had Israelites in mind, and Moses knew this. That was why he placed his life on the line for them severally, which eventually cost him his place in the Promised Land. When the people committed grievous sin he interceded for them and vehemently stood in the gap, preventing God from wiping them all out at once:

> *Now it came to pass on the next day that Moses said to the people, "You have committed a great sin. So now I will go up to the Lord; perhaps I can make atonement for your sin." Then Moses returned to the Lord and said, "Oh, these people have committed a great sin, and have made for themselves a god of gold! Yet now if you will forgive their sin-but if not I pray, blot me out of your book which you have written."* - Exodus 32:30-34

Responsibility and **accountability** are equally vital in the kingdom leadership pattern. As a leader, Moses was responsible for the people. He had a task to accomplish and the task was to take the people from where they were to where they were meant to be; leading them from a stale position to a better, well-articulated and defined destination. Any leadership that cannot achieve this is defective and ineffective. Apart from being responsible for the people, Moses was also accountable to God. He had to lead right; following God's instructions every step of the way.

These principles were also evident in the leadership style of Jesus Christ, who became responsible for the sin of humanity and was accountable to God every step of the way. We can also see them in the lives of successful leaders such as David, Nehemiah and a host of others. This leadership pattern is expected of this new generation. They will not only practice it, but also transfer it to others, thereby entrenching the standard of God in the world system until this age is brought to a close.

Their leadership style will also be characterized by the ability to birth new ideas in the earth. They will not repackage or recycle activities and programmes in competition with the world, but will pioneer new things with creative ability and ingenuity that will be acquired through apostolic wisdom and intelligence. God will release grace to conceive and implement innovative ideas to these emerging leaders. The society will do well to listen to these emerging leaders.

Some pastors are so desperate to keep the people in their fold and attract many more, that they now bring Babylon into their gatherings and programmes. It is rife to see posters and handbills in Nigeria with all manner of comedians and jesters invited to minister to the people. The idea is like rather than lose the people to the world, let's bring the world to them in the church. This is one of the ways some of our church leaders borrow strategies from the world rather than depend on the help and leading of the Holy Spirit to build the people and bring them to maturity. As demoralizing as it might sound, Nigeria still occupies an important spot in God's global purpose.

NIGERIA IN GOD'S GLOBAL PURPOSE
What God is doing in the 21st century is no doubt a global phenomenon, and different nations in the world have their unique roles to play. Different national peculiarities will be used to display God's manifold wisdom in this season. Nigeria as a nation equally has an important part to play in this.

Nigeria is the most populous Black Country, famous for being one of the most corrupt nations in the world, where majority of its people live below the poverty line. It is also a country that is richly blessed and yet annoyingly poor; poor infrastructural development, poor human capital development, and lopsided wealth distribution resulting to widening gap between the rich and the poor. These and many more negative labels are easily ascribed to Nigeria. This same country has the potential for greatness that can match and possibly surpass current superpowers.

Nigeria is in this present state today simply because of bad leadership, and the ever increasing disregard for kingdom values and principles. Even the leaders have admitted that our problem is that of leadership. And it is obvious that the leaders lack the capacity to do the right thing even when they know the right things to be done. The Nigeria we have currently is far from what it should be. This is the time for the Nigeria that exists in the heart of the God to emerge. The plan of God at this point is for the sleeping GIANT to arise and take its place among great nations of the world. Nigeria will be great again if we are prepared to make the required sacrifice.

Nigeria is one of those geographical expressions that God will use as the epicentre of what He is doing in the earth today. This may not be evident at the moment, but the word of God has gone forth and a people are emerging that will bring it to pass.

> *If My people who are called by My name will humble themselves, and pray and seek My face, and turn from their wicked ways, then I will hear from heaven, and will forgive their sin and heal their land.* 2 Chronicles 7:14

When the people of God in Europe in the 1500s and America in the 1600s responded to the demands of the spirit, those regions equally experienced socio-economic and political transformation. These were the periods of great revival and advancement of God's purpose in those parts of the world. They became the centre point of global economic and political activities. Most of those societies are currently facing various challenges of varying degrees, because they have abandoned the values and principles of the kingdom with which they were built.

Systemic and structural collapse will continue as long as the people continue to deviate from the principles and values of the Kingdom. A society where greed, injustice, and corruption reign with impunity, cannot experience development of any form. Nigeria's potentials would become a reality if we abandon our selfish and self-centered ways, and embrace the ways of God. The possibility of the socio-economic transformation is not so much as to make Nigeria a super power in itself, but to display God's manifold wisdom, so *"... that the living may know that the Most High rules in the kingdom of men, gives it to whomever He will, and sets over it the lowest of men"* Daniel 4:17.

ACTIVATION OF THE CYRUS DIMENSION
The Cyrus dimension is a pattern of God's operation in the earth where individuals who are not 'recognized', 'acknowledged' or 'perceived' as godly people are strategically used to advance His purposes in the earth. Cyrus was a heathen ruler of a heathen empire, who became the king of Babylon at the time of the captivity of the children of Israel. Prophets Isaiah and Jeremiah prophesied about him and what he would accomplish for God ever before he came to the scene, after the reign of Darius (Daniel 6:28).

His assignment, as prophesied by the two prophets, was two-fold. The first was that God made him His battle axe to bring judgment on erring nations. We must appreciate here that nations are not restricted to geographical delineations, but include belief systems, value systems and mindsets that inform how people live (Jeremiah 51:20). The second one was to set God's people free from captivity and to rebuild the ruined city of Jerusalem (Isaiah 44:28).

Activation of the Cyrus dimension in this season would be the emergence of individuals and leaders who are not necessarily "Christians" or religious in anyway, but would advance the purposes of God in Nigeria. It is erroneous and shallow to think God is only the God of "Christians". He is the sovereign God of the whole creation, including planetary systems that are yet to be discovered. God is not Christian and He does not have a religion, neither did

He give us any. He sent Jesus Christ to show us the way back to Him, and to set up the Church, which is the completion of His plans for humanity.

Those who subscribe to the values and principles of Jesus Christ are designed to make a difference in the world, particularly in system that have become rotten, only if properly equipped. There many instances where non-Christians have boldly stood against corrupt practices and other forms of evil, while some of our brethren are part of the perpetrators, and some others would rather fold their arms and watch for fear of persecution.

It is important for those who would work with God at this critical time to understand His heart and ways. It is erroneous to think God is sentimental along religious and ethnic lines like we are. He is the sovereign God who has jurisdiction over humanity and entire creation. He can do anything and no one can question Him. We need to have our hearts aligned with His in order to work with Him accurately in this season.

CHAPTER TWO

AN ARMY FOR THE FINISH

Anytime God wants to achieve something new in the earth, or take His people to the next level on their journey, He tends to look out for individuals or people with a different mindset to get it done. By this I mean individuals with the capacity to birth His will and purpose in that season. Jesus Christ noted in Matthew 10:17 that new wine is not poured into an old wine skin, but into a new wine skin. Vessels who are not 'full of themselves', and can empty themselves of old positions and experiences are poised to be used by God for new tasks. We can track this mode of operation in the Scripture. One of the earliest examples we can see is that of Joshua, which I love to refer to as the Joshua generation.

Moses led the Israelites out of Egypt, but Joshua was the one who led them into the Promised Land. Although Joshua was tutored by Moses, and served as his assistant, they belonged to different generations in terms of task and mode of execution. It is indisputable that God carried out astounding exploits through Moses in the course of the exodus from Egypt. Liberating the Israelites from slavery was actually his life's purpose, which he executed to the very best of his ability. However, when the journey was going to take a new turn, which was going to be characterized by a different kind and set of challenges, God decided to change the leadership.

We can argue that what happened when Moses struck the rock twice rather than speak to the rock (Numbers 20:1-12) was responsible for the change in leadership. While that is correct, we must also realize that everything will always fall in line with God's purpose. Even without the incident, God would have still changed the leadership for the next phase of their journey in as much as He found it necessary. The next phase in this case had to do with entering and conquering the Promised Land. Joshua emerged and took the people across, marking the end of their entire wilderness experience.

Another example is that of Gideon. When God decided to end the seven years of captivity of the children of Israel in the hands of the Midianites, He chose the most unlikely person to lead the army of Israel to war. When the angel of the Lord appeared to him to deliver the message, his response reflected the fact that he was the most unlikely person for the assignment in the natural:

> *So he said to Him, "O my Lord, how can I save Israel? Indeed my clan is the weakest in Manasseh, and I am the least in my father's house"*- Judges 6:15

At the end of the day, Gideon conceded to God and began his assignment right there among his people. He started by confronting idol worship and restoring accurate worship of God; he destroyed the altar of Baal and rebuilt that of God. It was after winning the internal battle against wrong worship system that he set out to deliver the people from the hand of the Midianites. In our day, it is mentalities and thought patterns that have hitherto opposed and challenged kingdom positions in the lives of the people. The Emerging Remnants will be somewhat confrontational in their approach, in a bid to correct wrong mindsets and paradigm among believers. All this will certainly be preceded by restructuring of their own individual lives. They will have to win the battle in their individual lives first before setting out.

The third example we will be looking at is our Lord Jesus Christ, who is the greatest Reformer in human history. Over 2000 years ago, God needed to bring about a great reformation that would set man on the path of restoration, and a return to His original intention. To achieve this enormous task, God had to 'create' a prototype in the person of our Lord Jesus Christ. Jesus as a man had a different spiritual *DNA*. He was the pioneer (first born) of a new species of human race (which was what God intended from the beginning, but was corrupted). Jesus Christ was the perfect blend of divinity and humanity.

> *For whom He fore knew, He also predestined to be conformed to the image of His Son, that He might be the **first born** among many brethren.* - Romans 8:29

When Christ came, the religious custodians of that generation were there; the Pharisees, Sadducees and the Scribes. But God decided to by-pass that entire generation because they lacked the capacity to navigate the next level. The religious leaders at that time had become blind and complacent and could not be used by God in anyway except to facilitate the death of Jesus Christ, which was orchestrated to pave the way to redemption. They ignorantly killed the Messiah they were anxiously waiting for. Their hypocrisy and religiosity had blinded them. Jesus was the new, they were the old and they did all they could to fight and destroy that which was new. History is currently repeating itself as some people have taken the Pharisees' position to oppose that which God is doing in our day, rather than submit themselves.

God is doing something new again in our day, and He is raising a new generation of people to accomplish it. He is building an army to facilitate the execution of His end time agenda from this present generation. The earth will once again be amazed by the manifestation of this emerging host who will not fit into the prevailing spiritual environment of popular Christianity.

RECRUITMENT

> *And it shall come to pass in the last days, says God, That I will pour out my spirit on all flesh; Your sons and daughters shall prophesy, your young men shall see visions, your old men shall dream dreams.* - Acts 2:17

Enrolment into this army has started. There is a fresh outpouring of the Spirit, and only those whose lives are accurately aligned with God's purpose will come under this outpouring and be enlisted into the Army. Discontentment for the prevailing spiritual order and a longing for more of God is the trigger. There is also the need for a resolve to pay the price and make the required transactions in order to be enlisted. In some cases, it would require a radical severance from the prevailing spiritual order to embrace the new. And this will not be easy as it would be resisted by the old order.

After over a decade in this new spiritual reality, it is quite amazing how the Holy Spirit is going about achieving this. Aside local assemblies that are aligning themselves this reformation, God is also singling out some individuals strategically. Some of them may not understand what is happening immediately, but in the process of time they will come to full understanding of everything. For these ones, there will be a fresh thirst and hunger in them that will not be satisfied by the prevailing spiritual environment. They will know deep inside that there is something more than just being born again and waiting to escape to heaven. They will know deep inside that there's a higher purpose to engage with here on earth, beyond having their needs met, and competing for fame and fortune.

The devil is aware of what God is doing, and knowing that this is going to be detrimental to his reign in human life, he will not just sit back and let things work out smoothly. He is going to put up some resistance. He will try but will equally fail to thwart God's intent for man in this season. He has been the enemy of man from the start; he does not want man to assume the state God intended. He was there before the beginning; made an appearance in the Garden of Eden. He was also there in the time of Jesus Christ and the time of Martin Luther in the 1500s. He is also aware of what is happening in our day.

If the devil was present to thwart the purposes of God during these historic times, we must not expect him to fold his arms and let things work out smoothly in our day. The devil is perfectly aware of his end; he has been judged by God already and his end has been determined. What he is doing however is to buy time for himself, which man does not have infinitely, because we currently exist in TIME. Jesus Christ acknowledged this when He said: *"I must work the work of He who sent me while it is day; the night is coming when no one can work"* – John 9:4. It is important we make the most of the time we have here and now to discover, do, and accomplish God's purpose for humanity.

The major opposition we are confronted with is with the recruitment process. There are two main dimensions to this. The first is the religious spirit that has crept into the Church, and the other one is the world system (Babylon). The most rigorous of these obstacles will come from within the Church. These people will have to cross this great hurdle to be enlisted into the Finishing Army; they will have to break down religious walls, barricades and impositions.

The Spirit of Religion

The spirit of religion that has pervaded the Church is posing a great resistance to what God is doing currently. The pre-occupation of most believers is not in line with God's plan in raising an end time army. Religious spirit has made majority of believers become complacent, and not able to access the intents of God for this season and beyond. As a result, people are locked up in wrong frequencies and religious walls. Those who are supposed to be shaped into a fighting unit are kept as babes and being spoon-fed. Apostle Paul described this situation in the book of Hebrews when he said:

> *For though by this time you ought to be teachers, you need someone to teach you again the first principles of the oracles of God; and you have come to need milk and not solid food. For everyone who partakes of milk is unskilled in the word of righteousness, for he is a babe. But solid food belongs to those who by reason of use have their senses exercised to discern both good and evil-* Hebrew 5:12-14

All these reflect in certain operational systems in the Church, which do not have the capacity to birth the purposes of God in this season. These operational systems include emphases and structures, which are responsible for the result we see in our society, vis-à-vis the advancement of the Kingdom of God in the earth. This brings to mind the question of the relevance of the church in our society today. The question that often comes to mind is why so many local assemblies, so many "Christians" and yet our society is in so much darkness? Millions of people are recorded in annual gatherings across the country, yet, corruption, greed, injustice and other social ills are widespread. The pertinent question is what are they being taught? What do they hear from our pulpits?

Apparently, believers are not properly trained and equipped for total kingdom life. What the average believer knows is what is taught at converts' classes. The Bible Study sessions are structured in such a way that the believer is merely exposed to religion rather than kingdom life as exemplified by Christ. Programmes and services are more of ritualistic practices to keep the people busy, rather than transformational initiatives. For instance, Paul made it clear in Ephesians that the saints are to do the work of the ministry which most are ill-equipped to do:

> *And He Himself gave some to be apostles, some prophets, some evangelists, some pastors and teachers, for the equipping of the saints for the work of the ministry for the edifying of the body of Christ, till we all come to the unity of the faith and of the knowledge of the Son of God, to a perfect man, to the measure of the stature of the fullness of Christ, that we should no longer be children, tossed to and fro by every wind of doctrine, by the trickery of men, in the cunning craftiness of men of deceitful plotting...* Ephesians 4:11-14

Young people have become the worst hit, as we are also confronted with the effect of doctrinal extremities. The two major prevailing extremes are legalism and absolute liberty. Young people who are trapped in the former operate and live under strict regulations which act to impede their access to and execution of divine intents. These are those who concentrate so much on the *don'ts,* which is common with the law that they end up not accomplishing anything for God or fulfilling their destiny. These ones find it difficult to give expression to the nature of God in them. These are good Christians who don't get to make exploits or contribute to kingdom growth. To most of these people, they are more conscious of the devil and sin, than they are of truth and God.

The other extreme of absolute liberty is equally detrimental. These ones express so much freedom in the Christian faith that it becomes difficult to differentiate them from unbelievers. These are *believers* who want to live like the people of the world. This is common with Christian youths who have become so modernised that they begin to manifest the works of the flesh consciously or unconsciously. They want to be in the Kingdom and yet hold on to Babylon. *For what relationship has righteousness with lawlessness; light with darkness; Christ with Satan; believer with unbeliever; temple of God with idols?* (2 Corinthians 6: 14-15).

To most people in this latter category, the line between kingdom lifestyle and worldly lifestyle has become blurred. That is why you visit some Christian youth gatherings and you are confused as to whether you are in the midst of reveling unbelievers, because modesty and caution even in dressing have been thrown in the wind. These people get so caught up in frivolities that they also end up not fulfilling divine intents for their lives and generation.

With these two extremes, nothing can be achieved for God in this season. Striking a balance and becoming accurate in God is of utmost importance, which is why the present reformation that emphasizes paradigm shift and the emergence of a new breed of believers is of the essence.

What makes this type of opposition difficult to surmount is not just because it operates within the religious structures of Christianity, but because it operates through the leadership. It is subtle and difficult to detect. It has all the trappings of accurate worship externally, but very weak and misalign internally. Its external posture is imposing and intimidating, so much that it cannot be questioned, not even in the face of the truth of the word of God.

That is why it's able to lock majority of the people in. This was the spirit that operated through the Pharisees in Jesus' days (Matthew 3:7; 5:20;23). Little wonder Jesus Christ repeatedly warned His disciples about them as much as He did about the world.

The World System (Babylon)

Babylon is a term used to describe the world system that is devoid of the principles and values of the Kingdom. When David wrote in Psalms, that 'I was born a sinner' (Psalms 51:5), he was referring to this system. It is the system we were all born into and are also required to come out of. It is like the matrix, the movie. It defines for man a form of life that is not real, and in opposition to the ways of God. That is the system the devil presides over as a prince or a ruler (John 12:31; 16:11). Anyone who subscribes to the values and principles of this system in the clutches of the devil.

Babylon has always and will continue to oppose the purposes of God. Its ways are different from the ways of God. Its operating system is totally anti-Christ. The world system conditions man to live in defiance to the values and principles of God. It defines for them what life is and how to live it, which is diametrically opposed to the intent and the design of God. It has the trappings of what one would call the "good life", and young people are the main targets because they form the most productive sector of the population of any society; they are full of energy and zest which the devil always wants to take advantage of. That is why the Preacher admonished:

> *Remember now your Creator in the days of your youth, before the difficult days come, and the years draw near when you say, "I have no pleasure in them".* - Ecclesiastes 12:1

The main weapon the devil uses here is deception. People are cajoled to believe his lies. That is why most young people think they have all the time to live as they please, in the process of which they engage in all sorts of risky behaviour. Most often than not, this perception of life leads them to their early destruction, and ultimately denies them access to the life of God. The end product of this strategy of the devil is to shut out as many people as possible from the purposes of God for their lives. In order for the devil to succeed sometimes, he ensures they exit earth without accessing the redemption Christ secured for all through his death on the cross.

Lusts in Babylon

There is nothing in the way and manner life is organized in the world that gives room for godly living. From birth, man is inundated with issues that border on survival. The urge to meet this need becomes the first consideration and underlining factor for other things in life; sometimes, choice of a career, a life partner, business venture, where to settle down, and sometimes how to relate with the Creator. A conscious effort is however required on the part of man to reconnect with his maker in the midst of these complexities, making His purpose the determinant of everything else.

Aside the need for survival, which has lured many people into making wrong choices in life, people are ensnared by subtle destructive value systems promoted by the entertainment industry. People buy into what they hear and see without knowing how far those things take them away from God. Young people now dine with the devil in order to satisfy these perceived needs the enemy has made them believe would fill the vacuum in their hearts, which can only be filled by God and nothing else. Most young people now allow what they see on satellite cable channels and the social media to define their lives. The moral fabric of the society is fast giving way as a result. The summary of it all is:

> ... *all that is in the world – the lust of the flesh [craving for sensual gratification] and the lust of the eyes [greedy longings of the mind] and the pride of life [assurance in one's own resources or in the stability of earthly things] - these do not come from the Father but are from the world [itself]* – 1 John 2:16 (AMP)

The energy young people possess is the same reason why the devil is always after them. In his effort to thwart the purposes of God for their individual lives, and then the ultimate purpose of God, the devil often picks on the best of the best for his own purpose. The devil, through the structure of the world system (Babylon), recruits the finest and the most intelligent and resourceful young men and women, some of whom he uses to advance his cause, while some others are rendered ineffective for God. The subtlety with which he perpetrates this makes it difficult for people to realize it. This is because to them, they are living their normal lives, not taking into account what or who is responsible for directing the course of their lives.

God is exposing religious spirit and the strategies of the enemy that seek to inhibit the emergence of the ultimate generation that would take His purposes to the next level. Some, particularly young people across the world have started asking the right questions. God is steering up the hearts of some, particularly young people, who are starting to question the way things have turned in the Church, and are seeking answers in God. As the barrier to accessing God in this light is broken, it is important for us to submit ourselves for training and equipping in order to function effectively in this season.

NEED FOR TRAINING AND EQUIPPING

At the end of every military recruitment process, successful candidates usually go through a period of training. This is when they are equipped with the necessary tools and strategies of defence and assault. The Finishing Army will also go through this process. The difference, however, is that the sum of their life experiences is part of their training. This is very important to the entire operation without which it would be practically impossible for them to function. This training is going to be in different dimensions.

The first dimension of the training is in the values and principles of God as contained in the Word. The end time soldiers will encounter the five-fold gifts of Apostles, Prophets, Evangelists, Pastors, and Teachers for a wholesome impartation. It is however not a coincidence that God has, in this season, restored completely the offices of the apostles and the prophets to complete the five-fold governmental gifts, through the Apostolic and Prophetic Reformation of the Church. The five-fold ministries are very important in the equipping and training of the end time soldiers (Ephesians 4:11-15).

The training will include the understanding of the times that we are in and the Apostolic doctrine. There will be the unfolding of the mysteries of the Kingdom. The soldiers will be trained and equipped to enable them withstand the wiles of the enemy, and birth the purposes and intents of God in the earth. Paul admonished his mentee, Timothy, to give himself to the study of the word (2 Timothy 2:15). There is granting of access into greater depth of understanding of the word in this season. And this will not be mere milk of the word, but solid food. Those who are used to soothing, emotional-laden and ego-stroking messages will not find this palatable. God is helping us breakthrough the religious strong-hold that keeps the people as babes and stunted.

The other dimension of the training and equipping of the end-time soldiers is in the world system. This includes the formal and informal training/education they receive and will receive in the society. The soldiers will have to understand that whatever it is that they are being trained for in the world would give them access to impact the system. We are expected to function like Daniel, Hananiah, Mishael and Azariah, the Hebrew boys that were schooled in the Babylonian educational system, in order to function effectively in Babylon.

The training and skills the soldiers will receive in the society are very important for them to be effective. Just the way Daniel displayed great intellectual prowess, so will the soldiers in their different fields of endeavour. Training, in this case, is not just the formal educational system; it also includes skill acquisition in different fields, and other informal trainings. If

Daniel and his colleagues had not been good at what they were trained at, it would have been difficult for them to make great impact in Babylon. God is not raising dummies, but smart and intelligent people who are being shaped into His image and likeness. While it used to be rife for those who are smart and intelligent in the natural to have nothing to do with God. That will no longer be the case. Although, most of them will not make it to the limelight, because they will not be competing for fame and fortune like the others that have been swayed by Babylon.

Aside these forms of trainings, they will also go through what I call the training of life. There will be trials to test the genuineness of their faith and resolve, and to also show them different aspects of the Father. The trial here is the Greek word *dokimazo*. It is the trial that is approved by God to test our faith. Peter said those who suffer according to the will of God should commit their souls to Him in doing good as to a faithful Creator (1 Peter 4:19). There is no stipulated time frame and limit to this training, as it is a continuous process. This is imperative because understanding is not complete without practical demonstration or experience.

"I hear and I forget; I see and I remember; I do and I understand." - Chinese proverb

CHAPTER THREE

BASIC FEATURES

Military personnel are known to have certain distinctive and outstanding characteristics that differentiate them from civilians. Their posture and attitude to life is usually different. Their organizational structures maintain a centralized command system; they do not break ranks, and are highly disciplined. They are also known to be resilient, focused, determined, and execute orders with high level of precision and accuracy. They live a regimented life which ensures they are always prepared for any assignment, and the successful execution of such assignments is always paramount in their mind, even at the expense of their lives.

These characteristics account for why they are always prepared to die in the course of defending their countries against internal and external aggression. All these and much more also apply to the soldiers God is raising in the 21st century. Some specific characteristics of the end time soldiers include, but not limited to the following:

Willingness to Journey with God
Any valid walk with God is a journey and not just a static religious experience. It is a journey of discernable and consistent transformation. The movement of the Israelites from Goshen in Egypt to the Promised Land is symbolic of this journey. God Himself is in charge, dictating the direction and pace of the movement. The Israelites' journey was characterized by a lot of events, which were meant to transform the people and bring them to a position where they would **know God, understand Him** and **become like Him**.

Although most of them died as a result of disobedience (because they were not learning and changing), there was no record of any tribe that decided to stay back and settle in the wilderness. In their journeying experience, they had about forty two encampments which would have been an opportunity for anyone or tribe to stay back. If that had happened, such a person or persons would have remained on their own because the presence of God would have moved on with the rest of the people.

The finishing soldiers are going to engage in a similar journey with God till they *breast the tape*. The finishing line will be very paramount to them that they will not want to stop on the way or settle for anything less. The destination of this journey is however not a geographical location, but a state of affairs in human life and the earth as a whole. One of the features of the destination is the establishment of the Kingdom of God on earth, which will culminate into the kingdoms of this world, becoming the Kingdom of our Lord and His Christ - Revelation 11:15. How exciting it would be when everything is brought under the authority of Christ.

The destination of the journey also speaks of immortality. A state when time as we know it would cease. And those who have been successful on the journey would step into timelessness or eternity. It is that point when *this corruptible puts on incorruption, and this mortal puts on immortality. So when this corruptible has put on incorruption, and this mortal has put on immortality, then shall be brought to pass the saying that is written: "Death is swallowed up in victory"* (1 Corinthians 15: 53, 54). We will not retreat, nor surrender.

Another depiction of the finishing line of this journey is Christ-likeness. We are all journeying into the person of Christ (Ephesians 4:15,16). The hallmark of this journey is a visible transformation in the life of everyone. Therefore, anyone who is not experiencing spiritual transformation which becomes manifest through their character, personality, and behaviour cannot be said to be engaged in this journey.

> *Behold what manner of love the Father has bestowed on us, that we should be called children of God! Therefore the world does not know us, because it did not know Him. Beloved, now we are children of God; and it has not yet been revealed what we shall be,*

but we know that when He is revealed, we shall be like Him*, for we shall see Him as He is. And everyone who has this hope in Him purifies himself, just as He is pure* (1 John 3:1-3) (Emphasis is mine).

For me, this is the greatest significance of the death of Jesus Christ. There is nothing in this world that can be compared to becoming like Jesus Christ, who perfected the blend of humanity and divinity. For this joy that is set ahead of us, the end time army will endure the process.

Submission to Process

Our understanding of who God is determines how we relate with Him and His purposes. While some people with a skewed view of God think He's always into quick fixes (instant miracles and all), He is largely strategic, deliberate, and takes us through processes for us to be able to do and become what He wants. In the same vein, God is going to take His soldiers through a process that will prepare them for the task at hand.

No country recruits soldiers, and immediately thrusts them into battle without taking them through series of rigorous and specialized trainings. This process is usually not just to prepare them physically, but mentally, psychologically, and otherwise. Whenever God has an important assignment for an individual or a people to execute, He takes them through a process of preparation. It is rigorous and tough because it is not appealing to the flesh. It takes the resolve to die to self in order to submit to this process. It is usually not a bread and butter experience.

Nevertheless, the grace of God abounds for all only if we do not lose heart and give in to short cuts (alternatives) the devil presents. It is this process that will determine our capacity to fight successfully in the course of the battle. All that is needed to make this seemingly rigorous process easy is willingness, determination, and the understanding that God is using it to build us up in preparation for what is ahead. That is why people lose heart whenever they cannot see God in the difficult situation they are passing through. The process usually kills the flesh but strengthens the spirit-man and properly aligns it with the Spirit of God. The greater death to self we experience, the more alive our spirit becomes. Here are a few examples of the people God used in their days, who had to submit to divine process.

David did not emerge as the great warrior king of Israel in one day. He fought many battles in his personal life. He passed through rigorous processes. Even before he was anointed king, he had fought with bears and lions while keeping his father's flock. This aided him to confront and defeat Goliath single-handedly. He also served under King Saul, who made several attempts on his life. He passed through all these before emerging as the warrior king of Israel. These processes taught him patience and dependence on God, among many other important lessons.

Joseph who became a great *Economist* and a *Prime Minister* in a foreign land (the land of his affliction – Genesis 41:52) went through a process before getting to that position. David, in making reference to him (Joseph), affirmed that *the word of the Lord tested him* (Psalm 105:17-19) before he began to fulfill the purpose of God for his life. You can take a moment to reflect on what it feels like to be the most favoured and loved in a large family. And for all that to change, by the hands of those you love and trust the most. Through his process, he experienced betrayer, temptations and possible 'short-cut' out of servitude, which he refused to settle for.

Jesus Christ also went through a process. He started His ministry at the age of 30, which lasted for about three years. All the years before His ministry started were for preparatory process. He had to learn and understand the books of the law. He studied to understand what had been written concerning Him. As the Son of Joseph, the carpenter, it is believed that He would have learnt the vocation of His father during that period. Despite the fact that He was God, He did not come to the earth in His majesty and glory, but came down in flesh and blood to demonstrate to us that we can live the life of God on earth. Jesus Christ had to go through about three decades of processing (Hebrews 5:8).

The processing of the finishing soldiers will be all encompassing. It will be spiritual, psychological, emotional, intellectual, etc. Every aspect of life of the soldiers will be checked and necessary restructuring will be carried out. It is through this process that those that will stand in the course of the battle will emerge. Every little detail of our lives will have to be given attention to, because they are all connected in order to bring us to where God has destined for us. Areas of life left unattended to would remain weak points the enemy would want to attack from, which makes it imperative to all God do the fixing.

> *He will sit as a refiner and purifier of silver; He will purify the sons of Levi and purge them as gold and silver that they may offer to the Lord an offering in righteousness.* - Malachi 3:3.

When this process starts, it is possible not to know that God is at work. Our whole life's experiences will be part of this process, including those we themed good or bad. All of our life's struggles, challenges, up moments and down moments are to make us strong and fit for the battle ahead of us. The process is also embedded with series of tests we will go through to prove our resolve and readiness. The successful ones at the end will be able to say:

> *For You, O God have tested us; You have refined us as silver is refined. You brought us into the net; You laid afflictions on our backs. You have caused men to ride over our heads; we went through fire and through water; but you brought us out to rich fulfillment.* – Psalm 66:10-12

The essence of this process is ultimately to produce the nature and character of God in us; a process of getting rid of the fallen nature we inherited from the first Adam. Before the advent of modern technology, gold refiners could only ascertain a refined gold when they saw their reflections through it. God is using the same technology in our day. The degree of the success of this process is the degree to which our lives reflect the nature and character of God.

Radical for Christ
This phrase has been used by different individuals and groups in the Church for different purposes, particularly by young people. A closer look at the adjective, 'radical' exudes its true meaning. Oxford Dictionary defines the word as *thorough* and *complete*. It also means *new, different,* and *likely to have a great effect*. All these words rightly describe the new generation that is emerging. The army will be made up of people who would be thorough and complete in Christ. They can simply be regarded as a new and different species of human race on earth, because they will be at the forefront of human civilization, in terms of level of conformity to the nature and character of God.

The radicalism defines their uncompromising nature, rather than extremism resulting to godless behaviour as seen in various parts of the world today. This nature will make them stand for what is right and just in their daily living. This tenacity and doggedness is important in order for them to fulfill the intents of God. It will help them confront the weapons the devil is deploying against the people in this end-time. While the world would increasingly become worldly, these soldiers would increasingly become godly, raising the bar of righteousness in every area of their lives, in contrast to prevailing order.

We must be aware that the greatest weapon of the devil, as we navigate towards the Finish, is DECEPTION. This strategy of the devil must not be toyed with. In the beginning, he (devil) started with deception - when he deceived our progenitors (Adam and Eve) to disobey God. That major thrust of the devil brought the entire creation to this present state of deprivation, decadence, backwardness, deterioration and death. He is using the same strategy in this end time, but with greater subtlety.

Through his cunning, he shall cause deceit to prosper under his rule; and he shall exalt himself in his heart. He shall destroy many in their prosperity. He shall even rise against the Prince of princes; but he shall be broken without human means. – Daniel 8:25

And he deceives those who dwell on the earth by those signs which he was granted to do in the sight of the beast, telling those who dwell on the earth to make an image to the beast who was wounded by the sword and lived. – Revelation 13:14.

Jesus Christ also warned us sternly about this when He said: *"For false christs and false prophets will rise and show great signs and wonders to deceive, if possible, even the elect."* - Matthew 24:24-25. God is opening the eyes of the saints to know that the presence of signs and wonders is the proof of God's approval. We are not only to expect false signs and wonders, but also false christs. Heightened sensitivity to God's required standard through His word is of utmost importance. And this will not be farfetched because our spirits would have been made alive and properly aligned with His Spirit.

With this in place, the end-time soldiers are expected to stand completely in Christ. They will stand for truth and righteousness. The deception of the devil would also be designed to make the saints compromise at different points in their walk with God, and any little compromise would give the devil an opportunity to cause much damage. This is where their radicalism for Christ would cause them to take their stand.

Do you not know that a little leaven leavens the whole lump? (1 Corinthians 5:6). It is important to guide against seemingly harmless compromises, as they could result to breaking of the hedge, thereby giving the enemy an opportunity to strike. This does not mean there would not be moments of weakness, but we must braze up immediately, fix whatever is broken at whatever cost and move on with God.

Death to Self

This is an important feature of the Emerging Remnants. No one can do great exploits for God without dying to self. Part of the nature man inherited from the fall is selfishness. Man became naturally self-centred; with greater consciousness of self rather than of God and His purposes. As a result, God was ceased to be centre of man's life. This made man become naturally rebellious and resistant to the will and purposes of God.

Conversely, it has become necessary to die to that nature in order to be able to do God's will and live as He wants us to live. Only those who have put the flesh (self) under can do the will of the Father. This is because the flesh is persistently antagonistic to the will and purposes of God. That is why Jesus Christ stated that *self-denial* or hating self is one of the requirements for becoming His disciple:

> *And He turned and said to them, "If anyone comes to Me and does not hate his father and mother, wife and children, brothers and sisters, yes, and his **own life** also, he cannot be My disciple.* - Luke 14:26

The task before the emerging soldiers is an enormous one, which cannot be accomplished with the interference of love for self. The task involves placing importance on the desires of the Father far above personal desires. It requires hating oneself, which, in this context, simply means that God has to come first in everything we do. He must become the centre of our life's pursuits and engagements, where we are only satisfied and fulfilled when we do His will. It is a call to serve God with **total abandonment**.

For whoever desires to save his life will lose it, but whoever loses his life for My sake will find it. - Matthew 16:25

Apostle Paul was able to accomplish great things for God because he was able to overcome the barrier of self. This was so real to him that he said: *"For me, to live is Christ and to die is gain."* Philippians 1:21-22 (NIV). He had nothing else to live for at that point other than for Christ. He was dead to self and alive in Christ. Same goes for those that would bring the purposes of God to the finish. We will have to keep dying to self in order to succeed. He (Paul) also wrote to the Corinthian Church: *"I affirm, by the boasting in you which I have in Christ Jesus our Lord, **I die daily**"*. 1 Corinthians 15:31

Apart from Paul, other icons who serve as a pattern for the emerging remnants also overcame the seduction and limitation of the flesh. If Daniel, Hananiah, Mishael, and Azariah had placed higher premium on their lives, they would not have been able to birth the will and purposes of the Father in Babylon. These four were not the only Hebrew boys who were selected to serve in the king's court (Daniel 1:6). Others who loved their lives would have blended in with the crowd. They would have been too afraid for their lives to stand out. Such people, according to Christ, will lose their lives in the end.

In Daniel's own experience, the fear of the lions' den would have prevented Him from observing his devotion to God. He rather prayed openly so his antagonists could see. Hananiah, Mishael, and Azariah would have sheepishly bowed to the gold image when they were brought before the great king Nebuchadnezzar. They instead lost their cool because the king was asking them to do the impossible. Joseph would have simply allowed the fear of being thrown to jail or the pleasure of sin to get the better part of him. But he rather kept himself away from Potiphar's wife.

> *Then I heard a loud voice saying in heaven, "Now salvation, and strength, and the kingdom of our God, and the power of His Christ have come, for the accuser of our brethren, who accused them before our God day and night, has been cast down. And they overcame him by the blood of the Lamb and by the word of their testimony, and they did not love their lives to the death.* Revelation 12:10-11

OPERATIONAL TECHNOLOGY – STRAIGHT ROD

'Straight Rod' is a technology of identifying a bent rod by placing a straight one beside it. Professionals who work in structural engineering or welders can easily spot a bent rod that may not be suitable for a particular purpose which an untrained eye may miss. The easiest way to prove to such people that a rod is not straight is to place a straight one beside it. The straight one will undoubtedly reveal the defect in the bent one.

The earth is currently characterized by wrong and defective mindsets and value systems. Children are born in these conditions, and they grow up devoid of the accurate value system and moral guidance. The prevailing defective mindsets are what they are accustomed to. Even when you try to tell them that what they perceive as normal is abnormal, they find it difficult to believe or change. Rather, they see you as the abnormal person.

This is the situation in the world today, aspects of which already pervaded the religious structure of Christianity. People have come to accept as normal those things that should be frowned at. And the situation is not getting better, partly as a result of globalization. Some Christians have been swayed into some these practices, while others simply look away. The best some Christians have been able to do is complain, but have not been able to exemplify and project the accurate picture of what is right, which would have revealed the defect in the prevailing ones in the society.

Our willingness and ability to live accurately in the midst of wrong lifestyles will cause the people to see the defectiveness of what they think and believe is normal and right. We also have to overcome the pressure and temptation to be like everyone else in order to show them the alternative. The paucity of practical demonstration of kingdom life can be attributed to the longstanding misrepresentation of the life of God on earth, which is one of the things the emerging remnants will be correcting.

This is a time for practical and lifestyle Christianity, where we are required to do as much as we speak. Instead of struggling to prove that a prevailing lifestyle and manner of doing things is the counterfeit, we will simply exemplify the original; raising the banner of God's standard for all to see. Jesus Christ made this explicit when He said:

> *You are the salt of the earth; but if the salt loses its flavor, how shall it be seasoned? It is then good for nothing but to be thrown out and trampled underfoot by men. You are the light of the world. A city that is set on a hill cannot be hidden. Nor do they light a lamp and put it under a basket, but on a lamp stand, and it gives light to all who are in the house. Let your light so shine before men, that they may see your good works and glorify your Father in heaven.* Matthew 5:13-16

It is hypocritical when we cannot live what we profess or preach. If we cannot make obvious difference in the society, then we are not better than the Pharisees in the time of Jesus. This explains why the Church has not been able to make significant impact in a country such as Nigeria, where there is so much darkness. We have thousands of local assemblies and millions of 'Christians', yet Nigeria is plagued with injustice, poverty, greed and corruption, among many others. So where is the impact? Where is the relevance? In other words: where is the saltiness and the illumination?

The emerging remnants, using the technology of the *straight rod* will practically demonstrate the life of Christ on earth. They will lead exemplary lives, as they permeate every sector of the society, birthing the will and intents of God. They will point people to the Way with their lifestyle and shine as light in the midst of darkness. They will become a reference point (ground and pillar of truth-1 Timothy 3:15), and will manifest as salt and light in a tasteless and dark world, before time is brought to a close.

The reaction of the world to them will not be same across board. Some will be admired, others will be scorned, persecuted and taken advantage of. They must not expect the world to celebrate them, but instead expect to be hated for who they believe in and what they stand for (Matthew 10:22; 24:9). In the same vein, some others would see them and gravitate towards Christ. Collectively, that is when the mountain of the Lord's house would be exalted above other mountains, and those who desire to be saved would rush to it (Isaiah 2:1-4).

CHAPTER FOUR

THE TASK

The existence of an army is one of the main features of a modern nation-state. One of the tasks of this important formation is to defend their countries against internal and external aggression. The Finishing Army likewise has an assignment to accomplish - a purpose. Their primary assignment is to establish the Kingdom of God on earth. They are to fight the end-time battle that will bring about the final collapse of every stronghold that has hitherto opposed the will of God for humanity.

ESTABLISHING THE KINGDOM

The coming or the establishment of the Kingdom of God on earth will not take place without a fight. This is because there is an existing kingdom that is not of God in the earth. The existing one will therefore not easily give way for that of God to be established. The prince (Satan) of this world (John 14:30) knows that the establishment of the Kingdom of God would bring an end to his reign in human life and in time as we know it. Establishment of the Kingdom of God in the earth would also signal his total defeat and ridicule, because man would have attained the fullness of God he so bent on preventing.

It is important to clarify that the establishment of the Kingdom of God in the earth is that state where the conduct of human life is governed by the values and principles of God. This does not mean everyone would submit to the lordship of Christ, but those who have decided to follow would have attained the predetermined measure of the life of God in the earth, the glorious state the enemy does not want man to attain.

It is in this light that the end time battle would be fought in the earth for the entrenchment of the lordship of Jesus Christ. This battle is going to be between the forces of good and evil, taking place in various dimensions. The devil is going to intensify his effort to ensure that man continues to live in total disregard for the ways of God. But a people (end time soldiers) would emerge to forcefully live by the principles of God and entrench His will in the midst of this fierce opposition.

Christ taught us to pray thus: "May God's kingdom come and His will be done on earth as it is in heaven" (Matthew 6:10). That is the task of the Finishing Army. As daunting as this may seem, judging by the manner humanity is further deviating from ways of God, victory is assured:

> *...the seventh angel sounded: And there were loud voices in heaven, saying, "The kingdoms of this world have become the kingdoms of our Lord and of His Christ, and He shall reign forever and ever!"* – Revelation 11:15.

This pronouncement by the seventh angel is an indication of victory for the ultimate generation. We are already experiencing some of the indicators of the end. This is going to require a deliberate and conscious effort of those who are enlisting into this army. Everybody will see it happening; the gladiators will be fully aware of what they are involved in as this would characterise their everyday experience in their families, careers, businesses, jobs, professions etc.

Daniel, who is one of the icons of understanding the operations of the finishing soldiers, also talked about the establishment of the Kingdom of God when he interpreted the dream of king Nebuchadnezzar:

> *You, O, king, were watching; and behold a great image! This great image whose splendor was excellent, stood before you; and its form was awesome. The image's head was of fine gold, its chest and arms of silver, its belly and thigh of bronze, its legs of iron, its feet partly of iron and partly of clay. You watched while a stone was cut out without hands, which struck the image on its feet of iron and clay, broke them in pieces. Then the iron, the clay, the*

bronze, the silver and the gold were crushed together and become like chaff from the summer threshing floors; the wind carried them away so that no trace was found. And the stone that struck the image became a great mountain and filled the whole earth. – Daniel 2:31-35

In its interpretation, Daniel revealed that the head of gold represented the kingdom of Nebuchadnezzar himself, who was the most powerful earthly king ever. Other parts of the image represent kingdoms and empires that have risen and fallen after that of Nebuchadnezzar. The last and least of them, however, is still in existence - the present world order. Although, it is still making immense effort to increase in strength and in capacity, God has revealed that it is partly strong and partly weak, because it is a mixture of clay and iron (Daniel 2:41-42). Its destruction is sure and inevitable.

Daniel also spoke of what the stone represents:

And in the days of these kings, the God of heaven will set up a kingdom which shall never be destroyed; and the kingdom shall not be left to other people; it shall break in pieces and consume all these kingdoms and it shall stand forever. – Daniel 2:44

Daniel went further:

Inasmuch as you saw that the stone was cut out of the mountain without hands and that it broke in pieces the iron, the bronze, the clay, the silver and the gold – the great God has made known to the king what will come to pass after this. The dream is certain and its interpretation is sure. – Daniel 2:45

As stated earlier, God works in partnership with His people to make things happen on earth. This does not mean God cannot do without man (Luke 19:36-40, Matthew 3:9), but because of the privilege He has accorded man, it has become a matter of principle for God to partner with man to accomplish His purposes. This battle will not be a 'bread and butter' event, but a real battle - it is going to be confrontational. This is because the existing world order will not give way easily to the ways of the Most High. Below are some of the specific assignments these soldiers will carry out.

Representation

The Scriptures made it clear that we are not of this world, but here to represent the interests of Christ (2 Corinthians 5:20). The *World* in this context means a system of existence that is not of God. Christians as ambassadors are to represent their place of origin which is from the other realm (in God), all of which Christ represents and demonstrated when He was here in flesh and blood. Jesus Christ Himself made this clear when He was arraigned before Pilate:

> *Jesus answered and said, "My kingdom is not of this world. If my kingdom were of this world, My servants would fight, so that I should not be delivered to the Jews; but now My Kingdom is not here.* – John 18:36

The implication of this is that we are not to live like the people of the world. There must be a clear distinction between the two kingdoms. As representatives of God on earth, our value system and principles cannot be defined by the world system. We live in opposition to what is prevalent in the world around us, which is dictated by its prince – Satan. Our lives, pursuits, goals and ambition must not be defined by this realm, but by the word of God.

The immediate purpose of the finishing soldiers is to bring about accurate representation and presentation of Christ in the earth. Most of what we have today is misrepresentation. That is why Christianity has assumed a mere religious status rather than a way of life that should be evident for everyone to see, which could ensure a corresponding change in the society. This has now pitched Christianity side by side other world's religions.

The concept of Christianity was not coined by Jesus Christ or the disciples. It was coined by the people of Antioch who could not find a better word to describe the disciples of Christ. From their observation, the disciples were like Christ, because their attitude and behaviour showed that they had been with Christ (Acts 11:26).

This is not what we have today. The Church has assumed a new dimension different from that of the early Church. Christians are now identified by the fact that they attend Church programmes, bear a 'christian name', or even carry the tag line 'born again'. Emphasis is no longer on practical Christianity, which is the exhibition of the life and character of Christ.

The present misrepresentation of Christ was prophesied by Isaiah when he said:

> *Behold, My servant shall deal prudently; He shall be exalted and extolled and be very high. Just as many were astonished at you, So His visage was marred more than any and His form more than the sons of men.* – Isaiah 52: 13, 14

This passage speaks of the distorted image of Christ in the earth. As a result of the religious activities that have taken over the Church, there is lack of accurate representation of Christ. This is why unbelievers and atheists are having a field day. Some of them see Jesus Christ as a mere prophet, servant of God or another outstanding man in history, whereas He is the prototype of the new man. Paul rightly describes Him as the first born among many brethren- Romans 8:29.

So many things are happening in the Church today that are the direct opposite of the character and personality of Jesus Christ. This is where the distortion of the image of Christ comes from. One of the responsibilities of the finishing soldiers is to bring correction to this distortion, by accurately representing Christ in the earth. This will be facilitated by the apostolic grace that God is releasing at this time. This will bring fulfillment to the final verse of Isaiah 52 that states:

> *So shall He startle many nations. Kings shall shut their mouth at Him; for what had not been told them they shall see, and what they had not heard they shall consider.* – Isaiah 52:15

These soldiers will ensure accurate representation of Christ in every area of human life they would be required to function. People will marvel at what they will begin to see and know about Christ through them. The soldiers will represent Christ in every capacity because they will possess the mind of Christ (Philippians 2:5), and consequently do things the way He would want them done. These will be His true ambassadors on earth. And those doubting the possibility of this really happening will be astounded.

Possessing the mind of Christ means having the same attitude and nature Jesus manifested when He was on earth. With this, the end time soldiers will be able to do things the way Christ would want them done; approach issues in manners that will please the Father. For instance, when Christ was on earth, He never did anything without the approval of the Father (John 8:28, 29). None of His decisions contradicted the intentions of the Father. That is how the Finishing Army will operate, because they will not live for themselves but for the will of God.

Presentation

The flipside of their representative mandate is accurate presentation. These soldiers will be required to rightly present Christ to the world. Since there is a lack of accurate representation, there has also been lack of accurate presentation. You cannot present what you do not represent, just as 'one cannot give what one does not have'.

Jesus Christ gave a mandate that we should go into the world and preach the WORD (Mark 16:15). The Scripture also made it clear that Jesus Christ is the Word. This means that Christians are to present Jesus Christ to the world. It is evident that the accurate presentation of Christ is a paramount aspect of the life of every believer. What is however prevalent out there is grossly inaccurate.

Inaccurate presentation has caused a great damage to the body of Christ. Different people now lay emphasis on different aspects of Christ that suits them, instead of the whole package that is able to build the saints. This has brought about schism and sectarianism in what is supposed to function as one body. This is what has created a strong denominationalism in the Church globally, with great walls of separation. It is in the oneness of the body that accurate and effective presentation can be made. Jesus made this point when He said:

> *I do not pray for these alone, but also for those who will believe in me through their word: that they all may be one, as You Father are in Me, and I in You; that they also may be one in Us, that the world may believe that You sent Me* – John 17:20-21.

This shows that for presentation to be effective there must be oneness, rather than division. This is one barrier that the finishing soldiers will have to surmount in order to achieve accurate and effective presentation of Christ to the world. The wall of separation that denominationalism has erected will be destroyed, and a Church without walls will emerge. This is one of the areas where the Church constitutes a barrier to the recruitment process.

The early Church presents a clear opposite picture of the situation. By their oneness, they were able to produce a synergy that affected their presentation of Christ even in difficult situations. They were able to achieve much more for the kingdom by working together. Tremendous power was generated because they functioned as a strong and formidable unit.

> *Now the multitude of those who believed were of one heart and one soul; neither did anyone say that any of the things he possessed was his own, but they had all things in common. And with great power, the apostles gave witness to the resurrection of the Lord Jesus. And great grace was upon them all-* Acts 4:32-33.

Fulfillment of Prophetic Pronouncements

Sometimes, it looks as if the devil is winning the battle for the soul of humanity, but alas, everything is going according to the plans and timing of God. Everything that is happening today is as written and purposed by Him. The emerging soldiers will equally facilitate the fulfillment of every prophetic pronouncement meant for their day, as there are still a number of them to be fulfilled before this age can be brought to a close. Peter pointed out that:

> *...He may send Jesus Christ, who was preached to you before, whom heaven must receive until the times of restoration of all things, which God has spoken by the mouth of all His holy prophets since the world began.* –Acts 3:20-21

The Scripture says the second coming of Christ would be like a thief in the night (2 Thessalonians 5:2, 2 Peter 3:10, Revelation 3:3), and that the day and time He would come no one knows. As a result of this scriptural position, some believers are in a frenzy that Christ could come anytime, even right now, without paying attention to the signs of the times and those things that have to be in place. This shows that the average believer does not know or is not concerned about what the Father wants to accomplish in the earth before bringing this age to a close.

In as much as no one knows the hour of His return, it is important for us to know that there is no way Christ would come when so many things that were meant to precede His coming are yet to be fulfilled. Rather than wanting to get saved and escape hell, the end-time soldiers will be preoccupied with birthing the intents of the Father for His entire creation.

The desire to escape hell and go to heaven, which is not wrong in itself, has created the *escapist mentality* in believers. So many believers are waiting for rapture instead of seeking to know and to do the will and purposes of God in the earth. It is either they are ignorant or they are not concerned about the things that must precede the coming of Christ. It is important that we remain sensitive to the Spirit in order to decode those things that must be accomplished before the return of Christ. Some of the things that can be clearly seen in the scriptures are briefly discussed below to give us some ideas:

Heavenly Invasion – Revelation 11:15
When John was banished to the Island of Patmos, it was a death sentence. It turned out to be an opportunity for God to grant us insight into some of the events that will characterize the end of time. Although there has been a lot of a misinterpretation of these events based on different eschatological leanings, the revelations of John, nevertheless, provide us fragments of understanding into what would happen in the end.

There was a declaration at the blaring of the trumpet by the seventh angel that the entire world has become the Kingdom of our Lord and of His Christ - a colony of heaven. This simply means the world forcefully conforming to the governance system of heaven. This would be the final divine response and fulfillment of the prayer Jesus Christ taught us to pray in Matthew 6:10: *"May Your Kingdom come soon; may Your will be done on earth as it is in heaven"*.

Attaining Confluence (Unity of the Faith) – Ephesians 4:13
The fragmentation that characterizes the structures of the Church, as is evident today, is one of the things that will be fixed before the end would come. Jesus Christ is coming for a complete body (a Bride) that is not

disjointed or deformed in any way. This will not be attained by every believer but by a remnant that are in tune with God, and would serve as representative of all.

Everyone who is engaged in a valid walk with God constitutes a global company that God will bring into a confluent state. This does not mean there would be one Church government similar to what existed in the dark ages, but a state where our collective experiences in God would be synchronized, and where our emphasis would be Christ-centered. At this state, there would be unity of purpose, as against the current denominationalism, sectionalism and disjointed doctrinal positions.

A note of caution here for those who have built or belong to personalized empires, as they may not be able to access this dimension of the plan of God. Some of these people are like the Pharisees in the days of Jesus, who have become self-sufficient, self-indulgent and comfortable as a result of their empires. The walls of those empires will be difficult to pull down to ensure integration and singularity of purpose. What was intended for comfort, safety and preservation would become what would lock them out of what God is doing. It's like building high walls in a bid to protect yourself and your belongings, and, in the process, trapping yourself within those walls.

Jesus Christ prayed for us that we may experience such perfect unity, that the world will know that God had sent Him (John 17:23 NLT). Our unification, as briefly explained above, is not up for negotiation in bringing this age to a close. And this would require individual parts dying to self, submitting to the other and regarding the other person more highly than oneself (Philippians 2:3).

Completion of the Building (Body of Christ) – Matthew 16:18
One of the many profound statements of Christ is the one He made in response to the accurate revelation of His person that Peter had: "I will build

my Church and the gates of hell will not prevail against it". As noted earlier, God is engaged in a building construction, and we are that building.

God has used several illustrations in the Scripture to describe the building process He is engaged in with His Church. Some of these include Noah's Ark (Genesis 6:14), the Tabernacle of Moses (Exodus 25:8), the Temple conceived by David and built by Solomon (1 Chronicles 28:11), the prophetic temple Ezekiel saw (Ezekiel 40), etc.

All these constructions represent the dwelling and the presence of God in the Old Testament, which were symbols of the Body of Christ in the New Testament. Strict and detailed instructions were given for them to be built to specification. So also is the Body of Christ. It is a dwelling place of God, and His manifestation in the earth. The building of the Church must meet the specifications of God. He will not accept a product that is substandard, because He is coming back for a glorious Church that is without spot, wrinkle or blemish of any kind (Ephesians 5:27).

Manifestation of the Sons of God – Romans 8:19
There is a manifestation of sons that will set the entire creation free from bondage. Note that it is not only man that is confronted with the consequences of the sin of the first Adam, but the entire creation of God. Remember that the ground was also cursed after the fall because of man in Genesis (3:17).

Verses 20 and 21 of Romans 8 clearly states that "against its will, all creation was subjected to God's curse". But with eager hope, the creation looks forward to the day when it will join God's children in glorious freedom from death and decay" (NLT). Just like man, the earth is equally groaning to be delivered. The earth however seems to be groaning more than man which now manifests in incessant earthquakes, tsunamis, hurricanes, tornadoes, landslides, floods, etc., across the globe. The earth is convulsing, and this will continue until the full manifestation of the sons of God.

A closer look at these prophetic declarations that must be fulfilled reveals a connection to the dream of Nebuchadnezzar that was interpreted by Daniel (2:44), and the prophecy of Isaiah (2:2-3). Daniel told the king that God will set up a Kingdom that will never be conquered but will crush all others. Isaiah said in the last days, the Lord's house will be exalted above others, and people will flow into it to learn and walk in His ways.

A Standard for God to Judge the World – 2 Corinthians 10:6

God is just, and there is no unrighteousness in Him. God is preparing the finishing army to emerge as a standard and a witness with which He would rightly judge the whole world. When His judgment comes, there would be no room to claim ignorance of His required standard, or that what He asked for could not be attained by man, even though He remains the unquestionable One.

Jesus Christ already warned us that as it was in the days of Noah, so will it be in the last days (Matthew 24:37; Luke 17:26). This statement has several implications and significance. One of them is that Noah met God's required standard for his day. The Bible says Noah found grace in the eyes of God, which was the primary reason he was chosen. The Bible also says that Noah walked with God; he was just, righteous and blameless in his generation (Genesis 6:8-9).

He also obeyed God by building the ark. At the completion of the ark, God destroyed the rest of the people. His standard for that season was Noah. The ark was meant to protect more people than just his household, but the people had total disregard for the life he built in God. The completion of Noah's obedience was the finishing of the ark, after which the rest of the people were judged. "… and being ready to punish all disobedience after your obedience is fulfilled." (2 Corinthians 10:6)

Another example we can see in the Scripture was during the course of the journey of the Israelites from Egypt to Canaan. As a result of their persistent disobedience and difficulty, God wanted to wipe them out and start a new line of descent through Moses. But Moses intervened and would not let that happen (Exodus 32:7-14). We can deduce that Moses met and was God's standard in that instance. While the people were only concerned about God's acts, Moses knew and was concerned about His heart (Psalms 103:7). In the same manner, we also have a standard in our day that every one of us would be assessed. That ultimate standard is JESUS CHRIST. God now awaits a people that would meet this standard, which would in turn serve as evidence and judgment for the rest of the world.

It is important to note that what is contained in this chapter is not exhaustive of the assignments of the emerging soldiers. But going by what we have, it is apparent that there's a lot of work to be done in order to bring this age to a close. While there is a bit of emphasis on what we have to do, it is important to equally pay close attention to who we become in the process. At the end of this process, we would have become emptied of ourselves and filled with the nature and character of God. That is how God intends to walk the earth. As vessels, we have to empty ourselves for God to fill us with Himself.

CHAPTER FIVE

THE BATTLEFIELD

It is important to note that while God is, at this point, raising accurate leadership in the Church, the focus is mature and functional saints. Majority of these saints will function at the frontline (secular sphere), which is where the battlefield really is. That is where we have to conquer for the Kingdom. God is not raising "church folks" or a set of religious people, but a people who will function as priests and kings in the earth.

The representation and presentation of Christ, which are two important tasks of the saints, will be out there in the world, and not in four walls (buildings) erroneously referred to as the Church. Local assemblies are to serve as training and equipping centres for these saints to emerge. The primary place of functionality (after all the internal battles have been won), which is the battlefield, is in the world. The soldiers will permeate every sector of the system of the world, establishing the principles and values of the kingdom.

The battlefield will further be looked at in terms of their immediate environment and various fields of specialization and functionality in the world system.

Immediate Environment

The saints will begin operation in their respective immediate environments. The immediate environment includes their homes and respective families. People close to them will be the first to notice and feel the impact of their unique attitude and behaviour. The way they will react to issues around them will be different. There will be remarkable and significant difference between their old self and their new self. They will not have to broadcast it, but the people around them will know this. It will be evident to all, just the way it happened to the disciples in Antioch. There will be visible evidence of spiritual growth and maturity.

They will truly possess the mind of Christ and will stand out and make great impact in their environment. Their focus would be to please God, just as Christ did and would assume the posture of "I do nothing on my own but say only what the Father taught me… For I always do what pleases Him" (John 8:28 NLT).

By operating in this manner, the saints will create their own world in their immediate environment; a world whose ruler, president, and king would be God Almighty. They will hold firmly to the principles and values of the Kingdom, so much that anyone who comes to their world will have to play by those rules or stay out. This will be as a result of their uncompromising stance.

> *For the weapons of our warfare are not carnal but mighty through God for pulling down of strongholds, casting down arguments and every high thing that exalts itself above the knowledge of God,* ***bringing every thought into captivity to the obedience of Christ****…* 2 Corinthians 10:4-5

Some Christians are not taken seriously in their immediate environments because they have not been exhibiting the nature and character of Christ. They only wear the label 'Christians' or 'born again Christians', but do not live the LIFE. Such cannot impact their world and therefore do not constitute any threat to the powers of darkness.

The emerging saints will be icons that will set things in order in their respective families. They will shoulder the responsibilities of their families; bringing every opposing thought and position to the obedience of Christ. They will contend with and prevail against every contrasting position to the will and purpose of God.

Professional or Vocational Environment

There is currently the challenge of secular-spiritual life dichotomy among believers, where it is believed that the person in the work place should be different from the person in church meetings. The Emerging Remnants will lead a seamless and singular life. The principles of the kingdom learnt in their local assemblies would be exemplified in their various areas of endeavour. They will function like Daniel, Hananiah, Mishael, and Azariah in Babylon.

Daniel and the others were God's people, who subscribed to and lived by the values and principles of the kingdom before they were taken captive in Babylon. When they were specially selected to serve the king of Babylon, they received Babylonian training in order to function effectively. The entire set up of the training was to make them subscribe to the lifestyle of Babylon. Out of all the Hebrew young men who were picked, Daniel, Hananiah, Mishael, and Azariah were smart enough to know where to draw the line. They served in Babylon, but did not live by its values and principles.

In the same way the Emerging Remnants are also being equipped in the world in different forms and at different levels. Some are trained and functioning as artisans such as plumbers, carpenters, masons, etc. Others are professionals such as teachers, engineers, psychologists, sociologists, and doctors. While they will receive these trainings and function in their different fields, they will know where to draw the line in terms of the underlining principles and values that are not in line with the prescribed lifestyle of the Kingdom.

The major consideration for career choices in the world today is how lucrative a particular chosen career is, in terms of financial and material benefits. In other words, people acquire knowledge and skills for mere survival. This is particularly rife in our country where income is largely tied to a particular type of degree and certificate. Majority of the students in our higher institutions of learning today want the certificates in order to secure their three-square meals after graduation.

The Emerging Remnants will see things differently. Their training and skill acquisition in the world will be seen as tools for service. They will have an understanding that everything was given for a particular Kingdom purpose and not for the gratification of fleshly desires. They are the remnants that will understand that they have been bought with a price (1 Corinthians 6:20, 7:23). Their delight will therefore be in anything that will bring glory to God. These people will not merely work for money, but chiefly, to serve and fulfil purpose.

Those with enormous financial and material resources amongst them will equally understand the purpose for which they were given. They will function with the underlining principles of **stewardship** and **liberality**. The principle of stewardship is the understanding that everything is given in trust, while that of liberality is to deploy everything as directed by God, who gives us the power to make wealth. It is in this light that these soldiers will not hold on to any time-based resources tenaciously or use them for self-gratification, but rather use everything to accomplish God's purpose.

The various capacities they will serve in constitute their respective battlefield, where they will contend with opposing forces to entrench Kingdom values and principles. These soldiers will spread across different sectors of the society: public and the civil service, politics, business, etc. They will permeate different sectors of the society, thereby expanding the lordship of Jesus Christ, until Babylon is completely destroyed and time as we know it, is brought to an end.

The Bible recorded that Daniel and his three Hebrew brothers were ten times better than the other students in Babylon after graduation. This was because God empowered them for the exploit they had to carry out for Him.

> *As for these four young men, God **gave** them knowledge and skill in all literature and wisdom; and Daniel had understanding in all visions and dreams... Then the king interviewed them, and among them all none was found like Daniel, Hananiah, Mishael, and*

Azariah; therefore they served before the king. And in all matters of wisdom and understanding about which the king examined them, he found them ten times better than all the magicians and astrologers who were in all his realm. - Daniel 1:17, 19-20.

The Emerging Remnants are expected to identify their innate potentials, develop and perfect them for the work ahead (self-development). They have to consciously and deliberately develop competences. They will equally be graced with apostolic wisdom and intelligence to function. They will be equipped with the power to create, the ability to pioneer new things and set kingdom standards in their different fields of endeavour. This empowerment will not just jump on them but will be received and nurtured as they submit themselves to process.

King Nebuchadnezzar of Babylon knew the import of having resourceful people in his administration. He wanted the best brains to serve in his kingdom. And Babylon is the typology of the world system in which we are today. The world is always looking for the best of the best. In the midst of technological advancement and increasing liberal policies, globally, the best in various fields are being sought after. This quest for best brains will pave way for these soldiers to assume prominent positions, where they will be able to further entrench kingdom values and principles in their areas of endeavour. Even while it would be as if their intelligence is paving the way for some of them, they will know that the hand of God is behind the scene, so they don't become proud and lose sight of the bigger picture.

The emerging soldiers will be positioned not only to make micro impact; they will also make macro and systemic impact. Those who will function as leaders in their respective fields will redefine leadership. Kingdom standards will be exhibited in various leadership capacities that will reveal the defects in the prevailing trend. They will lead as Christ taught us to:

> *So Jesus called them together and said, "You know that in this world kings (leaders) are tyrants, and officials lord it over the people beneath them. But among you it should be different. Whoever wants to be first must be the slave of all. For even I the Son of man, came here not to be served but to serve others, and to give my life as a ransom for many.* Mark 10:42-45 (NLT)

This is the principle that characterized the leadership of Jesus Christ, and since He embodied the prototype of what mankind ought to be, the finishing soldiers will have to take after Him. He practically demonstrated this type of leadership when He literally washed the disciples' feet (John 13:5-15). He did this to teach us how to lead; by serving. Unfortunately, this act has been erroneously taught and practised out of context in the Church today. Some church leaders now practically wash the feet of their congregations for different reasons; some in order to "possess their possessions", and for some other unintended and weird reasons.

As the soldiers take up their positions of leadership in the system, they will live a life of service for the people under them and the society at large. What is common in our society today is leaders taking advantage of their followers, and exploiting them. But that will not be the case in any social formation where the emerging soldiers are in leadership.

They will also not define success as the world defines success. Success in today's world is measured in terms of fame and fortune acquired. While many of these emerging remnants will also be successful in this manner, they will not be defined by them. As noted earlier, satisfaction and fulfilment would be derived from the life of service and doing the will of the Father.

EMERGING REMNANTS IN NIGERIA

As mentioned earlier, there is a general acknowledgement that the major problem confronting Nigeria as a nation is bad leadership. Nigeria is a nation enormously endowed with both human and natural resources. However, the management of these resources has been a major problem, and the result is evident in the lives of the people. There is a growing poverty in the midst of plenty, and a widening gap between the rich and the poor. We have about 5% of the population controlling 80% of the wealth, while 95% struggles with the remaining 20% of the resources.

For decades, our nation has been battling with an appalling national image in the international community; there is a pending threat of secession and disintegration; corruption has risen to unprecedented heights; incessant ethno-religious crises and numerous other problems. These problems have been caused by self-serving leadership we have experienced for years. Most of these leaders have only been succeeding at enriching themselves and their cronies at the expense of the generality of the people. To make the situation worse there is dearth of church leaders who can boldly speak the truth to those in authority, even though some of them are poised to do so.

There is a common belief and saying that a problem known and shared is half solved. Unfortunately, that does not apply here. Everybody knows what the problem is, but there is no real commitment to provide lasting solution. The political elite who plunged the nation into this situation are now confused as to how to lead us out. There are lots of questions begging for answers. The solution is in turning to God. "If my people who are called by my name will humble themselves and pray and seek my face and turn from their wicked ways, then I will hear from heaven and will forgive their sin and heal their land" (2 Chronicles 7:14).

There is a manifold wisdom of God that is yet to be made manifest. Different nations of the world have risen and fallen at different times. Nigeria is yet to give full expression to the intent and purposes of God. The time is NOW for that to happen, because God is still in the business of doing what the carnal mind would regard as ludicrous. Paul captures it thus:

Instead, God chose things the world considers foolish in order to shame those who think they are wise. And He chose things that are powerless to shame those that are powerful. God chose things despised by the world, things counted as nothing at all, and used them to bring to nothing what the world considers important. As a result, no one can ever boast in the presence of God. – 1 Corinthians 1:27-29 (NLT)

In the midst of the growing darkness and confusion in the land, new standards will be set in different spheres of human endeavour. It is going to be like a parallel civilization, because the Emerging Remnants will operate with a different set of value system. Those who are smart will begin to subscribe to these standards, because anything that is built on alternate standards and principles will not have validity beyond time.

Changing Leadership Style
One of the unique things about the Emerging Remnants is that they will detach themselves from every generational string. Over the years, in this country, there has been a massive and encompassing generational transfer of defective mindset from the older generations to the younger ones. The new leaders will completely detach themselves from this defective mindset. According to Vernon McLellan, "The worst danger that confronts the younger generation is the example set by the older generation." A mental revolution is required to change this ugly trend.

Some people are already expressing pessimism about this generation; that they will be worse than the present crop of leaders that we have, and those in the past. Indeed, there are indications to that effect. It is believed that the situation will continue to degenerate. While that is not far from the truth, the Emerging Remnants will operate differently in the midst of a perverse generation. They will not tow the rebellious path of the older generation.

> *For He established a testimony in Jacob, and appointed a law in Israel, which He commanded our fathers, that they should make them known to their children; that the generation to come might know them, the children who would be born, that they may arise and declare them to their children, that they may set their hope in God, and not forget the works of God, but keep His commandments; and **may not be like their fathers, a stubborn and rebellious generation, a generation that did not set its heart aright, and whose spirit was not faithful to God**. (emphasis mine)* - Psalm 78:5-8

In the past, as we can observe in the Scripture, there are instances where God brought in leadership that was different from the ones that had been in existence. It is a common trend for succeeding leaders to take after their bad predecessors. But there were some who decided not to be like their predecessors, thereby changing the trend. One example is king Josiah of Judah (2 Kings 22). He was very young when he assumed office, but he did not follow the footsteps of his father, Manasseh, and grandfather, Amon, who ruled before him (21). He chose to follow the footsteps of his forebear, David. He restored true worship back to Judah (23).

David is another example of a leader who did not follow the footsteps of his predecessor, Saul. Saul was a king allowed by God, even though he was not His desire for the people at the time. He gave them (Israelites) because they asked for a king; they wanted to be like other nations. Saul turned out to be a terrible leader. His credential as a leader is documented in 1 Samuel 8:10-18. However, when David became king, it was a different experience for the people. He brought a transformation to the leadership style in Israel. Whereas Saul took from the people, David gave to the people (2 Samuel 6:19). He was a leader who had the people at heart. The Bible also described him as a man after God's heart. This is because he sought after and deferred to the will of God in everything.

These leaders brought about transformation and reformation in their days, in spite of what their predecessors instituted before they took up the mantle of leadership. They changed the face of leadership, and history has that to say about them today. This is what God has planned for Nigeria in the 21st century. There is going to be a great transformation in leadership; these leaders will be used to entrench kingdom leadership style that will change the course of this nation, and put her in her rightful place in the community of nations.

CONFRONTATIONS

This leadership transformation will be met with stiff opposition, particularly from those who benefit from the status quo. The new leaders will be confronted with many obstacles in their respective battlefields. This will be a battle between two kingdoms; two sets of values and principles. As much as this will be a spiritual experience, it will equally manifest in the physical in different forms. Entrenching kingdom values and principles in a world that already has its own parallel operating system will not be an easy task, but that is the battle in itself.

The Emerging Remnants will be confronted with seemingly impossible situations, where they will be required to compromise their stance. One thing is certain; a little compromise by any soldier will result to a total defeat by the enemy. For the soldiers to succeed, they will have to be thorough and firm. This is what will ensure victory for them as shown by those who have had similar assignments.

DANIEL

Daniel was confronted with a number of challenges in his days, most of which were in the line of duty. He was faced with seemingly impossible situations where he was to choose between his life and what he believed in. First, the enemies were going to make him drop his guard in order to disarm him, but he stuck to his gun – his impeccable character kept him. He was an epitome of integrity, discipline and honesty.

> *So the governors and satraps sought to find some charge against Daniel concerning the kingdom; but they could find no charge or fault, because he was faithful; nor was there any error or fault found in him.* – Daniel 6:4

The new soldiers will have to be extremely careful because their enemies will go the extra mile to ensnare them. In the case of Daniel, when his colleagues could not get anything to indict him, they decided to seek for an instrument in the system to achieve their aim. That was when he found himself in a situation that would have made him want to save his life, thereby compromising his stance. Jesus Christ warned that *"whoever desires to save his life will lose it, but whoever loses his life for My sake and the gospel's will save it"*. Mark 8:35

Daniel was presented with a choice of bowing to the pressure from his colleagues, and chicken out of the system, but he did not. He did not resign his appointment, but stayed back and stood for God. Moreover, there was no room to resign in such a system as it was an autocratic and authoritarian regime, and not democratic as we have in most parts of the world today.

The world system, which could be easily manipulated, gave his colleagues the opportunity to get him. They could not get him to make any mistake that would put him away, but they could manipulate the system to get him to offend the king and the state. As a result of his faithfulness and discipline with which he served, even king Darius was reluctant to execute him, but he had to comply with the ad hoc law that was targeted at Daniel.

At the end of the day, Daniel had enough courage to choose God rather than try to save his life. He was smart and courageous enough not to try to save his life, and God came through for him. As a result of this, there was a major shift in the earth that made wild lions, all of a sudden, become friendly, and they were unable to feed on Daniel. The same set of lions devoured the evil plotters when the king realized what they had done.

There is always a result at the end of every battle. The end result of Daniel's victory was the change of the entire system. By the obedience and steadfastness of one man, the operating system of an empire was altered, which brought about the entrenchment of God's principles and values during the reign of king Darius in Babylon, which was backed by a decree. In order words the constitution was altered because of Daniel:

> *Then king Darius wrote:*
> *To all peoples, nations, and languages that dwell in all the earth: peace be multiplied to you. I make a decree that in every dominion of my kingdom, men must tremble and fear before the God of Daniel. For He is the living God, and steadfast forever; His kingdom is the one which shall not be destroyed, and His dominion shall endure to the end. He delivers and rescues, and He works signs and wonders in heaven and on earth, who has delivered Daniel from the power of the lions.* Daniel 6:25-27

HANANIAH, MISHAEL AND AZARIAH

The trio of Hananiah, Mishael, and Azariah also had a similar experience as Daniel. They were equally faithful and unshaken in their resolve to stand for God. In their own case, a system was set up in Babylon that was completely in opposition to the God they believed in, and since they were not ready to compromise their position, the situation became 'the trio against the state'. It was just three slaves against an entire kingdom; a kingdom that was directly under the control of the most powerful king God ever permitted to rule the earth (Daniel 2:37-38).

There were just three of them physically, but they were not alone; the Almighty God, whom they represented, was with them. Their situation was more confrontational because it was a feud between them and the king. It was not a plot by any ordinary person. The king instituted a policy that was antagonistic to their belief. It was the king himself who set up the image and gave the command for everyone in his kingdom to worship it, with a death penalty in case of defiance.

The threat of being thrown into the burning fiery furnace could not make the trio change their stand for God. They were not going to try to save their lives; they were prepared to die for what they believed in. The king himself could not believe anyone could be so *stupid* as to go against his decree, so, he decided to give them a second chance. It was at this point that the trio made it clear to the king that they were not going to back down on their decision to hold on to their God. The instruction of the king was so absurd to them that they dropped all the protocols when they gave him their final answer.

> *Shadrach, Meshach, and Abednego answered and said to the king,* **"O Nebuchadnezzar, we have no need to answer you in this matter. If that is the case, our God whom we serve is able to deliver us from the burning fiery furnace, and he will deliver us from your hand, O king. But if not, let it be known to you, O king, that we do not serve your gods, nor will we worship the gold image which you have set up".** *Daniel* 3:16-18

They made their position very clear to the king that they would not worship his gold image. Apparently, they did not love their lives unto death when it had to do with breaking the principles of God. The king became indignant, and at the end made good his threat. In the end, these three were able to transform a whole system by their resolve to stand for God.

They believed God could deliver them. But in order to show the king that they were serious with the position they had taken, they added "but if not". This means even if God would not save them, they were not going to worship his gold image; they were ready to die. At the end of that whole encounter,

> *Nebuchadnezzar spoke, saying "Blessed be the God of Shadrach Meshach, and Abed-Nego who sent his Angel and delivered his servants who trusted in him, and they have frustrated the king's word, and yielded their bodies, that they should not serve nor worship any god except their own God! Therefore I make a degree that any people, nation, or language which speaks anything amiss against the God of Shadrach, Meshach, and Abed-Nego shall be cut in pieces, and their house shall be made an ash heap; because there is no other God who can deliver like this"* 3:28-29.

JOSEPH

Joseph was created to preserve a whole generation in his day. The journey to his greatness/place of assignment was however a tough one. Egypt, in his day, represented Babylon. Egypt and Babylon are concepts that describe the world system, which also represents a strange land or a land of sojourn for God's people.

Although Joseph had an idea of what would become of His future through his dreams, he never had an idea of how he would get there. In all of the troubles he went through right from the hands of his brothers, down to Egypt as a slave, he remained faithful to kingdom principles and values. He refused to defile himself with Potiphar's wife, in spite of her insistence and the possible consequences of turning her down.

> *But he refused and said to his master's wife, "Look my master does not know what is with me in the house, and he has committed all that he has to my hand. There is no one greater in this house than I, nor has he kept back anything from me but you, because you are his wife. How then can I do this great wickedness, and sin against God?* Genesis 39:8, 9

Despite the fact that Joseph, a common slave in Egypt, had risen to the position of a manager in his master's (Potiphar) house that did not make him become frivolous. He remained faithful to God and his master. What was most paramount to him was having a clean record with God. He was not going to break his stance with God to retain his position, not even at the risk of his freedom or life. As a result of this, God's favour never left. God remained with him everywhere he went, even when he was thrown into prison.

> *But the Lord was with Joseph and showed him mercy and He gave him favour in the sight of the keeper of the prison. And the keeper of the prison committed to Joseph's hand all the prisoners who were in the prison; whatever they did there, it was his doing. The keeper of the prison did not look into anything that was under Joseph's authority because the Lord was with him; and whatever he did, the Lord made it prosper. – 39:21-23.*

Another important point to decode from the life of Joseph, which the emerging soldiers will have to watch out for, is despite the fact that he was wrongly accused and jailed, he did not give up on his dreams and God. Joseph remained faithful. If he had behaved otherwise, he would have aborted the purpose of God for his life and his destiny. He remained focused. He did not lose sight of the purpose of God for his life. At the end, he was able to save the people of Egypt, his family and others in surrounding territories, by the economic structure he helped to build in Egypt.

> *The famine was over all the face of the earth, and Joseph opened all the storehouses and sold to the Egyptians. And the famine became severe in the land of Egypt. So all countries came to Joseph in Egypt to buy grain because the famine was severe in all lands. – 41:56-57.*

KEY PRINCIPLES FROM THE ICONS

From the lives of the personalities examined above, two outstanding principles can be deduced, which are very important to the operations of the Finishing Army.

Avoiding Defilement

One of the ways the devil will use to disarm and render these soldiers powerless is defilement. All the icons above knew they could not afford to defile themselves, and they fought to stay clean. It took a deliberate and conscious effort for them to be able to avoid it.

For Daniel, Hananiah, Mishael, and Azariah, what would have defiled them was the portion of the king's delicacies:

> *But Daniel purposed in his heart that he would not defile himself with the portion of the king's delicacies, nor with the wine which he drank; therefore he requested of the chief of the eunuchs that he might not defile himself.* – Daniel 1:8

The devil will always seek to defile the soldiers of God. This is because once he succeeds at that, they will be rendered powerless. Once a soldier is disarmed in battle, he becomes as powerless as a dead lion.

Joseph also had to contend seriously with the sort of defilement many great warriors have fallen for, through Potiphar's wife. He stood his ground and purposed in his heart not to yield to her request. He was smart enough to know what a little compromise could cost him. Since she was an object of defilement, Joseph stayed away from her completely. A little accommodation of the object of defilement could constitute a great danger to any soldier.

For Joseph, it was Potiphar's wife; for Daniel and his friends, it was food (the portion of the king's delicacies). In our day, it could be any of these and many more, especially mammon. The devil will explore the most subtle methods to cause defilement. Many strong men have fallen as a result of these tactics of the devil. Many more of these tricks will be invented in this season. We will prevail only if we keep our gaze on God, because our capacity to overcome is in Him and not in ourselves.

Counting the Cost – Being Resolute

Another principle that is deducible from the experiences of these icons is that they all counted the cost. This helped them to become resolute in their decisions. Daniel and his friends, in different situations, were able to see death as the last resort of the system they were up against. That was why they were not moved when they were all threatened with death. Daniel, in particular, made it clear to his opponents that he was not scared of dying:

> *Now when Daniel knew that the writing was signed, he went home. And in his upper room, with his windows open toward Jerusalem, he knelt down on his knees three times that day and prayed and gave thanks before his God as was his custom since early days.* - Daniel 6:10

The threat of death could not prevent these soldiers from standing for what they believed in. The finishing soldiers will operate with this principle in order to win their battles. Jesus Christ also made this principle clear to his disciples, and, by implication, to all believers:

> *For which of you, intending to build a tower, does not sit down first and count the cost, whether he has enough to finish it... Or what king, going to make war against another king does not sit down first and consider whether he is able with ten thousand to meet him who comes against him with twenty thousand? So likewise, whoever of you does not forsake all that he has cannot be My disciple.* – Luke 14:28, 31, 33.

CHAPTER SIX

THE EMERGENCE

...A people come, great and strong, the like of whom has never been; nor will there ever be any such after them, even for many successive generations... A fire devours before them, and behind them a flame burns... – Joel 2:2-3

At this point you must be asking the pertinent question: Where, how and when will these soldiers emerge? The truth is that they are already emerging. The appointed time for this to happen is NOW, across the earth. Some of the soldiers are aware already, while others are not. Others are at different levels of preparation.

Imbedded in the 21st century Apostolic/Prophetic Reformation of the Church is the preparation and equipping of the Finishing Army. This new move of God is a whole package that will launch the Church of Jesus Christ into new dimensions of operations and manifestation in the earth. The present reformation of the Church has the capacity to birth the purposes of God for the earth in this *Kairos*. It also has the capacity to raise the end time soldiers and equip them for the task at hand.

The training and equipping, which the present Apostolic Reformation is doing, is like a rebirth for anyone who completes the process. It is like being born again the second time. This process involves a total overhaul of the internal configuration of the individual, and, by implication, the entire people of God that are in tune with His current move in the earth. The process is like *de-orientation* and *re-orientation*; developing a new mindset and a new heart totally different from what they had previously. And this will remain a continuous process (Romans 12:1-2).

This process of continuous renewal is very important because that is what guarantees the capacity to accomplish God's end time agenda. Some of these Emerging Remnants are aware that something is changing in their lives; they are beginning to see things differently and also question some things about their current spiritual experience and environment. Some others are experiencing the feelings of dissatisfaction. They are developing a hunger and thirst for God, which their current spiritual environment cannot satisfy. Some would become disillusioned about the prevailing Church system. If such people can find their bearing, then they will be enlisted into the Finishing Army of God.

Anyone who is going through any of the experiences above, or similar experience, needs to pray and seek for the help of the Holy Spirit for clarity. The Holy Spirit is the spirit of truth, who is to lead us into all truth. Jesus Christ said, *"...when the Spirit of truth has come, He will guide you into all truth; for He will not speak on His own authority, but whatever He hears He will speak; and He will tell you things to come"*- John 16:13.

If those that fall into this category can put their feelings/flesh/sentiment aside, and allow the Holy Spirit to guide them, He will lead them to their destination. The Holy Spirit will also connect them to the right source, where they will be trained and equipped for the task that has been given.

It is important to be led by the Spirit, because there are so many counterfeit prophets and apostles out there who are looking for gullible people to devour. The Holy Spirit will not lead anyone to such people. Do not forget that by the nature of their character and lifestyle, you would be able to identify the true followers of Christ.

DOUBTING THE PRESENT REFORMATION OF THE CHURCH
"He testifies about what he has seen and heard, but how few believe what He tells them!" (John 3:32 NLT). It is disheartening that there are some in the body of Christ who still doubt the present Apostolic/Prophetic Reformation of

the Church. There are some who have rejected it outright, while others are not bold enough to make a stand for it. Either way, it won't stop that which is in the heart of God for His Church and the earth in this season.

This, however, constitutes grave danger for those who could have been part of God's end time agenda but refuse to make the necessary transactions. So many people would be trapped in waterless religious structures with wrong frequencies and emphases, just like what the Pharisees did.

> *How terrible it will be for you, experts of religious law! For you hide the key to knowledge from the people. You don't enter the kingdom yourselves, and you prevent others from entering.* Luke 11:52

The unbelief, rejection and attacks that characterize this move of God are not strange. It is like that with every great move of God. Majority of the people did not believe the greatest reformation God carried out in the history of mankind, which brought about the transition from law to grace. That move was pioneered by the greatest reformer of all time: Jesus Christ. The religious leaders and majority of the people in His day did not believe Him, but instead opposed Him. At the end, they plotted His death. They killed Him, but could not kill what He brought to mankind. He delivered to mankind the true identity of the Father and gave man an open access to Him.

The 16th century reformation of the Church pioneered by Martin Luther did not come without rejection and opposition from the prevailing order of the time. The leadership of the religious system in his day vehemently rejected and opposed it. The opposition was so fierce that it resulted in physical conflict between the two sects that emerged: Protestants and the Catholics.

These two events are recorded in history. One thing is however noticeable, irrespective of rejection and opposition, the former still gave way to the latter. That which is in the heart of God will always prevail irrespective of what man thinks or does to oppose them, because He rules in the affairs of men. We have equally failed to understand that God can annul or upgrade what He instituted, when the need arises or once it is no longer relevant.

> *Therefore, if perfection were through the Levitican priesthood (for under it the people received the law), what further need was there that another priest should rise according to the order of Aaron? For the priesthood being changed of necessity there is also a change of the law... For on the one hand there is an annulling of the former commandment because of its weakness and unprofitableness; for the law made nothing perfect; on the other hand, there is the bringing in of a better hope, through which we draw near to God.* Hebrews 7:11-12, 18-19.

> *For if that first covenant had been faultless, then no place would have been sought for a second. In that He says, "A new covenant," He has made the first obsolete. Now what is becoming obsolete and growing old is ready to vanish away.* Hebrews 8:7, 13

God is the Lead on this journey and we cannot dictate to Him how He is going to get us to our destination. Whenever He asks us to move, we get up and move irrespective of what we have built or are building. He is the Almighty. He dictates the pace and we are to follow. It will be a frustrating spiritual effort to lag behind God's schedule and timing. Lagging behind His agenda would expose us to wild beasts and harsh weather conditions of the wilderness. We have to strive to be where God is per time, i.e. His current emphasis.

It is worthy of note that there are remnants of church leaders (Apostles, Prophets, Evangelists, Pastors, and Teachers) who are committed to working with God in achieving His end time agenda in spite of the opposition, particularly in the midst of growing falsehood. These are courageous leaders who are committed to training and equipping soldiers for the task ahead. Some are already launching out, fighting the good fight of faith. And, for those who are disappointed in the Church, particularly in Nigeria, rest assured that the prevailing religious structure of Christianity, which is popular out there, does not reflect the true state of Church. The body of Christ is being built, and is in the process of being perfected.

THE CALL

Recruitment into this army is not for any particular sex, sect, class or group. The call is for everyone. In God, there is no discrimination or selection; everyone has equal opportunity before Him. In the words of Jesus Christ, Himself, it is "whoever" or "whosoever" (John 3:15, 16; 4:14; 11:26; Matthew 12:50). In essence, everyone is qualified for the call into the Finishing Army.

The most important thing is our response; the desire and determination to respond positively to the call. The younger generations that are in focus here make up the segment of the population that is too busy for God. Some of them have been sucked in by Babylon; serving the cause of the prince of this world. Some others that have been blinded by religion cannot access that which God is calling them into.

Those who have and will eventually answer the call must beware of DISTRACTION. This is one of the strategies the devil will employ in his attempt to thwart what God is doing. The devil will bring issues of life to distract these soldiers. They will have to be resolute like Paul when he said, "**Who shall separate us from the love of Christ? Shall tribulation, or distress, or persecution, or famine, or nakedness, or peril, or sword?**"- Romans 8:35. On the other hand, we must not allow comfort or wealth to distract us also. We must learn to maintain balance either way. Paul said, I have learnt to be abased and abound (Philippians 4:11-12).

The Finishing Army must overcome this strategy of the enemy if they are to accomplish purpose, and the earlier this is dealt with, the better. The reasons why this must be dealt with totally is that, first, the devil is employing this strategy in order to buy time. Distraction is to help him delay his day of doom. Secondly, if the devil succeeds with his plans to thwart God's purpose for our generation, we will lose out of our special place in God's end time agenda. This is because man operates and lives in time and space; man is limited by time, but God is not. Man can run out of time but God cannot. This generation must do everything possible to counter this strategy of the devil, so that God's purposes can be accomplished. What a great privilege and honour it would be to fulfill all that God wants in this season.

Although the task ahead looks tedious and seemingly impossible to accomplish, that is what God has created us for. If we align ourselves properly, we will have the capacity to accomplish it. It is however important for those who will answer the call not to be weary at any point, as the grace to reach the finish is available to everyone who is committed to the cause. We must not give in to discouragement. Jesus said, **"No one, having put his hand to the plow, and looking back is fit for the kingdom of God"** - Luke 9:62.

Confronting Discouragement
Aside distraction, we must be prepared to confront discouragement, particularly from the people close to us. There will also be events in and around us that will challenge our faith and stance. This is another strategy the devil will also employ to disarm and render us powerless.

We must be prepared for all manner of name calling as a result of our belief. We will be taunted and ridiculed, particularly as we will not be seduced by material wealth. But this will not and must not stop us, as our strength to succeed will not come from this realm but from God. We have the likes of Joseph, Daniel, Noah, Job, and many others to also learn patterns from. Although the task ahead is enormous, God is saying, "be courageous."

Joshua and Caleb had to confront discouragement when they were sent, among others, to spy on the land of Canaan. Ten of them brought back words of discouragement, but these two stood out and encouraged the people (Numbers 13:30; 14:6-9). When Joshua eventually took over the mantle of leadership from Moses, God said to him: "Be strong and courageous, for you will lead My people to possess all the land I swore to give their ancestors... I command you be strong and courageous! Do not be afraid or discouraged. For the Lord your God is with you wherever you go". Joshua 1:6-9 (NLT).

When David was handing over the mantle of leadership to Solomon, he also told him: *"...Be strong and courageous, and do the work. Don't be afraid or discouraged by the size of the task, for the Lord God, my God is with you. He will not fail you or forsake you..."* 1 Chronicles 28:20 (NLT).

Daniel, Hananiah, Mishael, and Azariah were certainly not the only Hebrews who were taken to Babylon, or chosen to serve the king. Out of all of them, these four chose to be different. They chose to stand out. I can imagine what their fellow Hebrews would have said to them. Although it was not recorded in the Scripture, Daniel and his friends must have been taunted when they refused sumptuous delicacies meant for the king, and settled for mere vegetables.

The Emerging Remnants must not allow discouragement to set in. We must stand firm in what we believe in. We must remain bold, courageous, and be comfortable with the exceptional life God has called us to live. Jesus Christ also admonished us thus:

> *And I say to you, my friends, do not be afraid of those who kill the body, and after that have no more that they can do. But I will show you whom you should fear: Fear Him who, after He has killed, has power to cast into hell; yes, I say to you, fear Him!* – Luke 12:4-5

Paul said to Timothy:

> *Endure hardship with us like a good soldier of Christ Jesus. No one serving as a soldier gets involved in civilian affairs – he wants to please his commanding officer.* – 2 Timothy 2:3-4 (NIV)

Personal Message

Dear Reader,

I am glad you spared some time to read through this book. It is important I let you know that significant advancement has been made in our journey towards the finish. Despite the numerous challenges confronting the Church, the intents of God are intact and are being fulfilled.

There has been a consistent movement of the remnants in our collective journey. If you have not been sharing in this experience, then it is because you have not been in tune with the current speaking and dealings of God with His people. Between the time the inspiration for this book was given and now, so much progress has been made, details of which cannot be contained in any single volume. The saints (remnants) across the world are experiencing tremendous internal shift and adjustment that is producing the nature and character of Christ in them.

Your attention is being drawn to this so that you do not think that this is all there is to know about the journey to the finish. This book has only attempted to provide fragments of insight into what God is doing in our day, which is still very much unfolding. We now know that there is no stopping (fossilizing) until we have become everything He designed us to be, and accomplish all His purposes for our lives and humanity.

Jesus Christ, in His response to Satan in Matthew 4:4, encouraged us to live 'by every word that **proceeds** out of the mouth of God' (emphasis mine). A people with insatiable appetite for the *proceeding word* of God have emerged, and, on a regular basis, are placing a demand on heaven for the next level in our journey back to Him. To these people, God has been speaking and will continue to speak, until this age is brought to a close. For those whose focus remains 'bread and fish', I only wonder if they will ever have their fill.

Also, there are some out there who have lost faith in the Church as a result of wrong emphases, doctrinal inaccuracies and practices; be informed that the Church of Jesus Christ is being built, as pointed out in this book. Some of you have even abandoned the assembly of believers. I will encourage you to find your way to emerging assemblies out there, where the current speaking of God, which is able to equip and transform you is being emphasized. These assemblies may not be popular, religious or laced with the usual paraphernalia of a "happening church", but be assured you will find the LIFE that your spirit is yearning for. This is a witness, because no excuse would be tenable before God if you missed your place in His Kingdom for the aforementioned reasons.

For those who have become dissatisfied with the prevailing spiritual environment, and are locked in religious strongholds, it is time to break free. These are individuals who are genuinely passionate about God but whose spiritual lives have been circular rather than linear. It is not a good experience to have so much hunger for God, yet be feeding on the same thing day in, day out. To express that in another way, it is spiritual torture to keep hearing the same thing (but packaged differently each time), when you are desirous of God and His will. That is what I call 'spiritual junk'. This cannot lead to maturity, but rather keep the people as babes. If this describes your present situation, then it's time to ask God for a new *sheepfold*, where you can be fed properly.

I pray that the Holy Spirit would lead you out of *pasturelands* without healthy *grazing,* to *sheepfolds* where you can grow, become and accomplish all that God intended for you. This is the time to take personal responsibility for your spiritual development, and beware of *wolves in sheep's clothing*. There are lots of *wolves* out there who are looking for materials with which to build their personal empires rather than build the people for God (Ezekiel 34).

God bless you!

Frederick Adetiba
www.frederickadetiba.blogspot.com
Email: fredor4c@gmail.com
Twitter: @fredor4c

I am excited to see the passion and drive of a young man like Fred towards a very deep understanding of the heartbeat, pulse and move of God in our day. It gives me great joy and hope for our generation.

I pray that he continues to function like the sons of Issachar in our time, and a channel for many to understand and rightly position themselves in God's current move in the earth.

Obiwon
Gospel Recording Artiste

Frederick O. Adetiba is an HRM practitioner and a Social Engineer/Researcher.

In addition to his professional practice, Frederick is involved in mentoring, community service and development, as well as advocacy for good governance.

He currently serves as a Secondary Leader at New Tribes Assembly, Abuja, a Reformation Kingdom Community.

Frederick loves God and he is deeply passionate about God's purpose for his generation, his country, Nigeria, and entire humanity.

Good book, good read, defining the parameters of operations of God's end time army. A must-read for anyone who senses a call into God's ultimate army. God bless you Fred.

Pastor 'Lere Agunbiade
Senior Pastor, Apostolic Grace Christian Centre, Jos, Nigeria.

A timely wake-up call to the Nigerian Christian community to its eternal purpose and earthly relevance. I couldn't think of a message and messenger more apt for the times. At once enlightening, deep and easy to read. This is recommended for anyone who wants to make a difference.

Tobi Oluwatola
Phd Fellow, Rand Corporation, California, USA.

This little book in your hand can make your entire life (priority, pursuit, emphasis) more precise, exact and accurately adjusted to line up with our destination. Fred takes us through the grasping of the context and content of the current emphasis of God, through the rudiments of the requirement to be enlisted in the army, to what the task ahead of us is, and where the battlefield really is.

Engr. Brendy Ndukwe
Senior Pastor, New Tribes Assembly, Abuja, Nigeria.

God is eternal. Therefore whatever God wants to do, He is already doing! Glory to God, Fred is not prophesying in the future tense in this book, but with great clarity and plainness of speech, removing the ever thinning veils shrouding the invisible realms to grant us access and insight into what God is doing right NOW! Tomorrow is NOW because prophecy is being fulfilled! This book will help us lean in, tilt our souls, to align with what God is already doing in His Church, of which we are members.

Ben Atuluku
Prophetic Speaker and Author, SpiritOutbreak Community, Abuja, Nigeria.

i-Change

www.ingramcontent.com/pod-product-compliance
Lightning Source LLC
Chambersburg PA
CBHW031420160426
43196CB00008B/1007